THE JOSSEY-BASS
BUSINESS & MANAGEMENT SERIES

DESIGNING AND LEADING TEAM-BASED ORGANIZATIONS

A Workbook for Organizational Self-Design

Susan Albers Mohrman

Allan M. Mohrman, Jr.

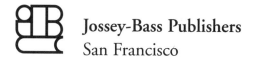

Jossey-Bass Publishers

San Francisco

Substantial discounts on bulk quantities of Jossey-Bass books are available to
corporations, professional associations, and other organizations. For details and
discount information, contact the special sales department at Jossey-Bass Inc.,
Publishers (415) 433-1740; Fax (800) 605-2665.

Jossey-Bass Web address: http://www.josseybass.com

Manufactured in the United States of America

Library of Congress Cataloging-in-Publication Data

Mohrman, Susan Albers.
    Designing and leading team-based organizations : a workbook for organizational
       self-design / Susan Albers Mohrman, Allan M. Mohrman, Jr. — 1st ed.
    p. cm. — (The Jossey-Bass business & management series)
    ISBN 0-7879-0864-9 (pb)
    1. Work groups. 2. Organization. 3. Management. I. Mohrman, Allan M.
      II. Title. III. Series.
    HD66.M634 1997
    658.4'02—dc21   96-48676

FIRST EDITION
PB Printing   10 9 8 7 6 5 4 3

CONTENTS

For
Weedie and Bernie
Lorraine and Al

HOW TO USE THIS DESIGN WORKBOOK

THIS BOOK IS A TOOL FOR DESIGN AND DIAGNOSIS OF TEAM-BASED ORGANIZATIONS

Designing and Leading Team-Based Organizations is a tool for managers, leaders, and design teams who are establishing or refining team-based organizations—organizations where teams carry out the core work processes.

It provides guidelines and principles for understanding the team-based organization and a framework for thinking through the design of such organizations. The design includes the team and organizational structures as well as the systems, processes, and behaviors that need to be put in place for team-based organizations to be effective.

The team-based organization is based on a new organizational logic. The time spent thinking through its design is an investment in developing the organization that fits your work—as well as an opportunity to develop a deeper appreciation of the new logic.

Some of the processes examined in this book—such as leadership, direction setting, communication, and decision making—are the bread and butter of all organizations. However, they occur in different ways in the team-based organization. These materials provide guidelines and examples and ask you to plan how these processes will occur in your team-based organization.

This book will be useful for

❑ Managers, management teams, and design teams that are designing a team-based organization.

❑ Management teams for programs, new product development, and other work where there is a recurring need to build team-based organizations for particular purposes and redesign them as work goes through phases.

❑ Management teams of existing team-based organizations that want to develop a deeper understanding of these organizations and their role in them, and that want to refine the design and improve the performance of their team-based organizations.

Team-based organizations exist at multiple organizational levels—and have to be designed at those levels. For example:

❑ A whole division of a company might be redesigned as a team-based organization. A management team or design team at the divisional or regional level can use this tool to examine the *macro* design of the business—the major business-unit groupings and the businesswide systems and processes—and to think through the issues involved in making it effective.

❑ A local management team or design team can use this tool to design each of the business units within the larger business, such as programs, product organizations, projects, mini-businesses, or units dealing with a customer set. Within a larger organization, different business units may need quite different designs in order to optimize the use of valuable human resources in carrying out the local work performed in each.

Ideally, a design team from the same organizational unit will work through these materials together to take advantage of multiple perspectives and broad knowledge of the work of the organization. For example, a management team or design team might use these materials to design or refine its team-based organization. The team should include people with all the key knowledge sets required to understand the work of the organizational unit. By working together through the design sequence, this core of people will develop a shared understanding of the organization. In some cases, an organization might want to use this tool as the basis for large-group design—involving all of the people in the organizational unit in thinking through these steps.

These materials might also form the foundation for educational sessions aimed at developing a deeper understanding of team-based organizations so that each participant can be a more effective manager, leader, or member of them. Even for educational purposes, it's best if sessions include multiple people from the same organizational unit. Much of the learning takes place through application—by examining your own organization in the course of doing the exercises in this book. These exercises work best if done with a group of participants.

THIS BOOK IS ORGANIZED IN MODULES

This book contains nine modules that take you through a systematic sequence of design steps. When you're finished, you'll have created a relatively complete framework for your team-based organization.

Each module includes

 Principles, rationale, and guidelines. Read and discuss these building blocks before you do the exercises in each module.

 Examples of design solutions. These examples are not prescriptive. They represent one possible design approach.

 Activities to guide you through the design process. You can do these activities on your own or as a group—or both.

 Some suggested next steps—things to remember as you begin to implement your design or make changes in your organization.

You can complete the design process in an intensive multiple-day session or in a series of sessions, each of which addresses one or more modules.

The discussion that accompanies the design tasks is essential to learning and to generating a good design. The design elements required to create an effective team-based organization are not quick fixes. They require the application of principles that have profound implications for how the organization operates and for the roles of people within the organization. It's essential that people talk about these implications and how to apply them.

We recommend that groups going through these materials for the first time use a facilitator. (A leader's/facilitator's guide is available.) However, the tools are designed to be self-guiding for groups that are more experienced with working in and creating team-based organizations.

DECISIONS YOU MAKE IN EACH MODULE BUILD A FOUNDATION FOR DECISIONS IN LATER MODULES

YOUR DESIGN SHOULD BE A LIVING FRAMEWORK

The modules are arranged in an order that has worked well in a number of company settings. When you follow this order, the design choices you make in the early modules can serve as a basis for later design decisions. For example, in Module 2, you create the team configuration that fits your work. Later on, you design communication and decision-making processes to fit those teams and support the work. The order doesn't mean that one aspect is more important than another. The team-based organization is a system, and all aspects support the others.

Design is not a linear process. As you move through the modules, you'll probably think of things that you forgot in earlier modules, and you may want to go back and modify or add to earlier work. You should think of the process as an iterative one. You can continue to modify and evolve as you learn, not only in this design process but also as you gain experience in your team-based organization. Learning organizations are flexible and continually examine whether they are organized for high performance.

Management and design teams will find that the work they do as they go through these modules is just the first step. A key to the success of a team-based organization is that all members understand the design, its principles, and how it's intended to operate. Disseminating the work of the design team and soliciting input from the organization's members is essential in creating a context for success.

FOR MORE INFORMATION

These materials are based on the team design model described in *Designing Team-Based Organizations: New Forms for Knowledge Work* by Susan Albers Mohrman, Susan G. Cohen, and Allan M. Mohrman, Jr. (San Francisco: Jossey-Bass, 1995).

More in-depth treatment of all the topics treated in this design tool are available in that book. It draws on four years of research examining teams in knowledge settings and many more years of research on teams in general. Much of the research was conducted at the Center for Effective Organizations in the School of Business Administration at the University of Southern California.

Designing and Leading Team-Based Organizations: A Leader's/Facilitator's Guide is also available to assist anyone leading a group through the self-design plan of this book.

ACKNOWLEDGMENTS

We received a great deal of help and support in preparing these materials. We are indebted to Kathi Vian, who helped move us from the linear world of the sentence, paragraph, and chapter to a format much more accessible for guiding design. Bill Hicks planted the idea of a short design book, and Cedric Crocker worked with us to bring it to fruition. Linda McKee, Tim Osking, Donna Robbins, and Paula Wynnwckyj supported earlier versions of the materials and provided extensive and invaluable feedback on how well they worked in Honeywell. Michelle Simon of the St. Paul Companies and Kay Quam of Synaxis provided many useful suggestions. We are indebted to production assistance from Alice Mark and Mike King.

Our work on team-based organizations has drawn on the rich heritage of organizational design knowledge generated by our colleague Jay Galbraith. These materials are based in large part on the learnings we gained in our long and enjoyable partnership with Susan Cohen. We are also indebted to the many corporations that participated in our research on team-based organizations at the Center for Effective Organizations at the University of Southern California.

THE AUTHORS

SUSAN ALBERS MOHRMAN is a senior research scientist at the Center for Effective Organizations, School of Business Administration, University of Southern California. She received her A.B. degree (1967) in psychology from Stanford University, her M.E.D. degree (1970) from the University of Cincinnati, and her Ph.D. degree (1978) in organizational behavior from Northwestern University. She has served on the faculty of the Organizational Behavior Department in the business school of the University of Southern California.

Mohrman's research and publications focus on innovations in organizational design processes, team-based organizations, high-involvement management, organizational learning and change, and human resource management. She has consulted with a variety of organizations, introducing innovative management approaches and redesigning structures and systems.

She is the author of many books and articles. Her books include *Self-Designing Organizations: Learning How to Create High Performance* (1989, with T. G. Cummings), *Large-Scale Organizational Change* (1989, with associates), *Creating High Performance Organizations: Practices and Results of Employee Involvement and Total Quality Management in Fortune 1000 Companies* (1995, with E. E. Lawler III and G. E. Ledford), and *Designing Team-Based Organizations: New Forms for Knowledge Work* (with S. G. Cohen and A. M. Mohrman, Jr.). She is active in the Academy of Management and serves on the review and editorial boards of several journals.

ALLAN M. MOHRMAN, JR., is a cofounder of the Center for Effective Organizations, University of Southern California. He was formerly on the faculty of the College of Administrative Sciences at Ohio State University. He earned his B.S. degree (1967) in physics from Stanford University, his M.A. degree (1970) in secondary education from the University of Cincinnati, and his Ph.D. degree (1979) in organizational behavior from the Graduate School of Management, Northwestern University.

Mohrman's major interests are performance management; organizational design, change, and learning; the design of effective systems for human resource management; and team-based organizations.

He is coauthor of *Doing Research That Is Useful for Theory and Practice* (1985, with associates), *Designing Performance Appraisal Systems: Aligning Appraisals and Organizational Realities* (1989, with S. M. Resnick-West and E. E. Lawler III), *Large-Scale Organizational Change* (1989, with associates), and *Designing Team-Based Organizations: New Forms for Knowledge Work* (1995, with S. A. Mohrman and S. G. Cohen).

GETTING STARTED

This module presents some of the key concepts that underpin the use of teams—especially the design and management of team-based organizations.

The logic that guides a team-based organization is different from the logic of a traditional, hierarchical organization. All in the organization need to think differently about how things are accomplished and about their own roles and responsibilities. People grow to think this way as they apply these concepts and try out new ways of doing things.

This module helps you make that shift. It clarifies the reasons for using teams and for designing a team-based organization. It explains the difference between traditional, hierarchical organizations and team-based organizations.

This shift of thinking is the foundation for the rest of the modules in this book.

ALL ABOUT TEAMS

WHAT IS A TEAM?

A team is a group of people whose work is interdependent and who are collectively responsible for achieving an outcome:

- ❑ Designing, developing, and/or producing products
- ❑ Delivering services
- ❑ Meeting the needs of a customer or set of customers
- ❑ Introducing improvements and innovations
- ❑ Integrating various parts of the organization

WHAT IS A TEAM-BASED ORGANIZATION?

A **team-based organization** uses teams to perform the core work of the organization—to turn knowledge and raw materials into products and services that customers value.

The whole organization is designed to create units consisting of the various contributors necessary to do a whole piece of the business.

Team organizations do much of their work laterally: people work with their peers in the team, and teams work with other teams to accomplish tasks and make decisions.

Some organizations use teams for special purposes, such as process improvement, but do the core work through their line-and-box hierarchy. These are not team-based organizations. They are organizations that use teams. For many organizations, this may be the best way to organize.

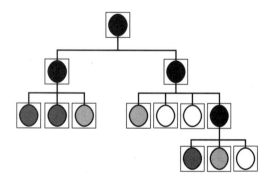

A hierarchical "line-and-box" organization

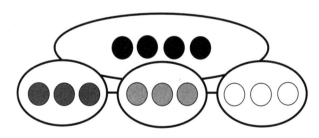

A lateral team-based organization

Caution: Don't generalize from past experience

You may have been a member of a team in a traditional, hierarchical organization. Don't generalize from that experience. Teams in a hierarchical "line-and-box" organization fight an uphill battle because the power structure and systems of the organization work vertically. Team-based organizations are designed to support the work of teams.

WHAT IS A HIGH PERFORMING TEAM?

In today's world, high performance is more than just getting the job done. A high performing team:

❑ Accomplishes its objectives efficiently and effectively

❑ Contributes to the effectiveness of the larger business unit

❑ Learns and then improves its performance through time

❑ Builds team-member commitment

Management must be willing to change the organization

Teams do much of the work that used to be done through the hierarchy.

Systems, roles, and procedures are changed.

Knowledge, skills, and rewards reinforce and support doing work laterally.

Leaders change the way they operate to deal with a team rather than one-on-one with subordinates.

MYTHS ABOUT TEAM-BASED ORGANIZATIONS

All organizations should be team-based
Plenty of organizations can divide work so individuals can work independently.

Everyone should be in a team
Even in team-based organizations, some work is not best done in teams.

All teams are the same
There will probably be many types of teams in an organization, and they will probably operate very differently.

Team organizations don't have hierarchy
Some teams manage the context in which other teams work. This constitutes a hierarchy of teams.

Teams don't need leaders
Leadership is required in all teams. Sometimes, more than one member is a leader.

Setting up teams is all it takes to create high performance
The entire organization must be designed to support teams.

Team-based organizations don't have managers
Everyone in a team-based organization has some role in managing it. But there are still pure management roles.

ALL ABOUT TEAMS *(continued)*

WHY TEAMS?

Companies use teams to respond to increasing performance pressures in highly competitive environments:

❑ To create collective focus on a program, a set of customers, a complete process, a problem, or an opportunity

❑ To integrate the work of people with different perspectives and competencies

❑ To generate innovative solutions by bringing diverse viewpoints and knowledge to bear

❑ To generate high involvement by creating a piece of the business for which a group of people has authority, responsibility, and accountability

❑ To save time and cost—decisions and approvals don't have to move through layers of hierarchy

WHEN IS A TEAM-BASED ORGANIZATION APPROPRIATE?

A team-based organization works best when:

❑ Work is interdependent, requiring ongoing integration of the knowledge and work of different contributors

❑ The organization can be divided into a set of units each of which can be given responsibility and held accountable for a piece of the business

---

Managers have a pivotal role

They lead the organization in a new way of operating—and remind others of the new logic whenever there's backsliding.

SHIFTING LOGICS

THE LOGIC OF TRADITIONAL ORGANIZATIONS

Combining people into functional units with similar tasks and knowledge makes the organization easier to manage, maintains functional effectiveness, and promotes efficiency.

Breaking work down into individual jobs and assignments promotes individual accountability and allows the organization to take advantage of specialized knowledge.

People get trained only in what they need to do their job.

Managers control, coordinate, and integrate the work of the people they manage, and are held accountable for the work of the unit.

Strategy formulation is done at the top of the organization. Control and implementation functions are in the middle. Executing of technical tasks is the responsibility of the nonmanagerial members of the organization.

Good managers "buffer" the technical core of the organization from the uncertain environment of the organization.

Innovation and improvement occur primarily through functional organizations.

Career growth is upward movement in the hierarchy.

THE LOGIC OF TEAM-BASED ORGANIZATIONS

Teams can focus attention on results if they're composed of all the skills and knowledge needed to produce a product, deliver a service, or carry out a complete process.

Ownership, commitment, and motivation increase if a team is given authority and responsibility for a whole piece of the business and is held collectively accountable.

The cost is lower if tasks previously carried out by managers can be moved into teams. Team members need business and management skills.

Teams can work more flexibly and effectively if people have some understanding of each other's work and if they have some cross-training.

Quality is higher and cycle time is lower if decisions are made, as often as possible, by teams whose members have the relevant information and perspectives—as opposed to decisions being made through the hierarchy.

Managers create the conditions for teams to be effective.

Innovation and improvement occur when people with diverse perspectives work together and find better ways to do things.

Career growth occurs through assignments that provide opportunities to develop broader and deeper skills and responsibility.

Beware—These two logics clash

At first, you'll have to keep reminding yourselves to act consistently with the new logic.

Backsliding is a natural tendency, especially when something goes wrong.

SHIFTING LOGICS:
WHAT TO DO

Start by developing a clear idea of why you are using teams. Everyone in the
team needs to have a common understanding: how teams fit with the work
and how teams can help you be successful. Take a few minutes to write down
your thoughts—individually and as a group.

SUCCESS FACTORS
What does your organization need to
do really well?
❑
❑
❑
❑
❑
❑
❑
❑

POTENTIAL BENEFITS

How might teams help achieve success in your organiza-

tion? Which of these general benefits is relevant to your

success factors? Explain how.

❑ Collective energy focused on overall results, such as

schedule, cost, quality, or customer satisfaction.

❑ Innovation—teams can come up with new

approaches to meeting business demands

❑ Speed—decisions made by those doing the work

❑ Development—people can learn new skills and

contribute more effectively as part of teams

❑ Quality—people take each other's work into account

and coordinate better

❑ What other benefits might you experience from a

team organization?

❑ Cost—fewer managers can focus on broader issues as

teams coordinate and manage their own work

WHAT'S NEXT

In this module, you've thought about what it takes for your organization to be successful and how a well-functioning team structure might contribute to effectiveness. Remember:

- ❑ You need to share this thinking with all members of the organization and get their thoughts and input.

- ❑ These benefits will come from teams only if the people in your organization work to be effective in the team organization.

You're just beginning your journey. The rest of the modules in this book will help you design and build your team-based organization.

TO DO

_____

_____

_____

_____

_____

_____

_____

_____

_____

_____

_____

_____

_____

_____

_____

_____

_____

_____

_____

_____

_____

_____

_____

_____

_____

_____

_____

_____

Don't expect immediate success

Everyone has to learn new roles and new ways of doing work. At first, it may seem that work takes longer and is harder to accomplish in teams. Success depends on persevering through the hard work of learning and start-up.

DESIGNING TEAM STRUCTURES

Team-based organizations systematically build in the ability to do work and coordinate work laterally.

This module provides a set of criteria and steps for designing team structures. Team structures are the skeleton of the team-based organization. They are designed to facilitate the work of the organization.

Team-based organizations have several different kinds of teams. Each involves a commitment of resources and must be carefully designed to add value to the organization.

The work of various teams may impact each other. The connections between teams must also be designed.

Team organizations must continually improve their organizational design and the work processes they use. Improvement teams can be established for this purpose.

In this module, you analyze the work system of your organization and determine an appropriate team structure.

 # TYPES OF TEAMS

TEAM PURPOSE

Team-based organizations are a set of business units and teams. Each contains all or most of the resources required to carry out its part of the work of the firm. Different teams have different purposes:

- ❑ **Work teams** perform the core work of the firm—they convert knowledge, labor, and raw materials into products or services that deliver value to the customer.

- ❑ **Integrating teams** coordinate and integrate work across the organization and/or across teams.

- ❑ The **management team** is a special kind of integrating team. It makes authoritative decisions about strategy, priorities, resource allocation, and organization for a business unit with multiple teams.

- ❑ **Involvement teams** are representative teams that perform tasks that were once the domain of management, such as coordinating the performance management process.

- ❑ **Improvement teams** plan and introduce changes to the organization to improve its performance.

Most team-based organizations have each of these kinds of teams.

Team-based organizations may also organize some of their competencies into **shared service units** that provide services—such as specialty consulting—to the work teams. Shared services may be interdependent teams, or they may be a group of people whose work is not interdependent and who perform their work primarily as individuals.

WHERE TEAMS REPORT

Teams may be the primary organizational structure, and all members may report to the team's leader, manager, or management team. All team members receive common direction from the same source.

Alternatively, teams may be *overlay* structures. Different members may come from different units. These teams have a more difficult time achieving focus because different members may be receiving different direction from their units. There is often a priority conflict among members.

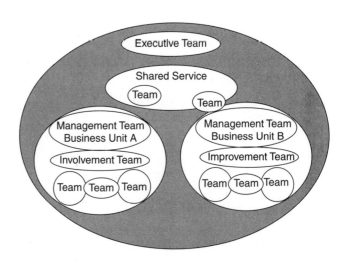

A team-based organization

TIME FRAMES

Teams may be permanent or temporary. For example:

❑ A permanent team may be set up to deliver services to all customers in a geographic area. The customers change, but the team is ongoing.

❑ Teams set up to perform a project are temporary. If the project lasts for a long period of time, the team may function like a permanent team.

Organizations with a large number of temporary teams face the challenge of moving people from team to team as the mix of activities changes. Even if a team is permanent, people may move in and out of it through time. New members can bring new ideas and revitalize a team. However, it takes time for a team to absorb new members, and team effectiveness may temporarily slip.

Teams need explicit approaches to bring in new members—ways to introduce them to team norms, operating processes, and expectations. The team should also be open to input from its new members.

If the work of a team-based organization goes through phases, the organization needs to review and change its team configuration over time. An example is an electronics program that begins with product definition and moves through stages ending in full-scale production. Of course, newly configured teams have to go through a start-up process.

Teams are composed of precious and limited resources. Organizations need to dismantle teams or change their configuration when the mix of work of the organization changes.

SKILLS AND KNOWLEDGE

Cross-functional teams contain members with a variety of knowledge bases and skills. Their members:

❑ Carry out team tasks that utilize their set of skills and expertise

❑ Coordinate and integrate work across functions

❑ Enhance organizational performance if team decisions take into account different functional or disciplinary perspectives

Innovative approaches are often generated when the team effectively combines the knowledge and perspectives of different members.

Cross-trained teams have members who have been trained in several skills and can carry out multiple tasks.

❑ A completely cross-trained team is one where all members can do all tasks.

Cross-training gives the team great flexibility in deploying its members to different assignments. Of course, complete cross-training isn't possible where several deep kinds of expertise are required to carry out the work of a team. However, the work of all cross-functional teams is facilitated if some members have overlapping competencies and everyone develops at least some understanding of the others' disciplines.

In addition to technical skills, team members need business and management skills and understanding—as well as good interpersonal and group process skills.

DEFINING WORK TEAMS

BASIC PRINCIPLES

The team configuration is based on an analysis of the work.

The design process starts with a clear definition of :

❑ The organization's mission

❑ The deliverables—its products and/or services

Knowing these helps identify the work that must be done and the skills that are required.

PROCESS ANALYSIS

Process analysis is a way of looking at the work of an organization:

❑ A process is the set of connected activities that delivers value to the customer, such as the development of a new product or the provision of a service.

❑ A subprocess is a subset of activities that constitutes a relatively whole piece of work and can be relatively self-contained.

For example, the development of the manufacturing processes for a new product is a subprocess of the new product development process.

A business unit, such as a new product development program, might house an entire process. Each team in the business unit might house one of its subprocesses. In this way, teams still do a "whole" piece of work.

Teams should be maximally self-contained. That means:

❑ Minimal crossing of team boundaries to accomplish work

❑ Maximal dedication of people to the team's work

❑ Maximal power of team to make decisions that affect its ability to get work done

To identify teams that meet these criteria, you have to look at your organization through three different lenses: process analysis, task interdependence, and decision interdependence.

TASK INTERDEPENDENCE

People are task-interdependent if their work affects each other.

❑ **Rule of thumb:** People who need real-time information about each other's work in order to adjust or complete their own work should be on the same team —particularly if the interface among them can't easily be routinized or programmed.

For example, individuals who are designing the software and hardware of an input-output device for an electronic instrument are task-interdependent. Changes made to the design of the software may impact the design of the hardware, and vice versa. Put the hardware and software engineers on the same team, if possible.

In contrast, service/repair people who each make individual visits to a daily list of customers are minimally interdependent. They work as independent agents, although they may have some interdependence if they share some scarce equipment. They can be organized into a work group rather than a team.

DECISION INTERDEPENDENCE

Most work involves a set of ongoing decisions and trade-offs that have to be resolved by the various parties whose work is affected by the decisions.

❑ **Rule of thumb:** A team should include the people required to make the ongoing decisions that affect the team's work.

For example, in the custom system development business, pricing involves an ongoing trade-off between revenue (more repeat business may stem from lower pricing) and profit (higher short-term profit results from higher pricing). Marketing, finance, technical, and business management all need to be in the same team in order to make this trade-off.

It's a creative process

Designing teams is a creative process. You analyze the work and determine a set of teams that perform a whole process —and contain the people who are task-interdependent and can make the key decisions required to keep work moving.

Usually, you can't get perfectly self-contained teams, so you have to make some judgment calls.

Take a look at the example of team definition on the next page. It illustrates how a business unit divides its work process into subprocesses and constructs teams that house most of the interdependencies.

CREATING A PROCESS MAP

Suppose you're analyzing a new product development (NPD) project with about fifty people, some of whom are only partially dedicated to the project.

You can use a high-level process map (below) as a process-analysis tool. On the left are the skill sets (disciplines) that have to be applied in the NPD process. The map itself portrays the way tasks relate to each other over time as the product moves from concept to design to manufacturing and then to distribution.

IDENTIFYING INTERDENDENCIES

The arrows in the figure below show the process flow of information and output among tasks. They therefore indicate some of the key task and decision interdependencies.

This analysis reveals three major task clusters of key interdependencies. These clusters can be identified with integral subprocesses:

❑ Design subprocess

❑ Manufacturing process development subprocess

❑ Sales, distribution, and logistics subprocess

Note that, in this example, full-scale manufacturing is carried out in a different division that has its own teams.

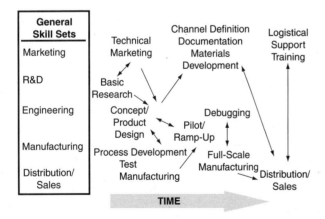

This high-level process map shows one way to illustrate the process of new product development

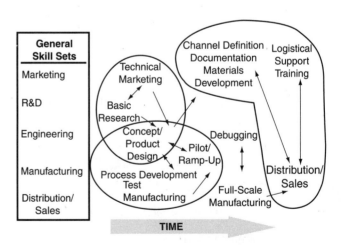

The map can show the interdependencies and clustered components in the new product development process

CONFIGURING THE PROJECT TEAMS

Building on the rough breakdown of work teams in the previous step, you can create the actual team organization as shown to the right.

All members of work Teams I and II are fully dedicated to the project. Some are members of both teams and provide cross-team integration. Team III also services other NPD projects. Its relationship with Teams I and II can be well specified so overlapping membership is unnecessary, although the technical writer in Team III acts as a liaison to Team I.

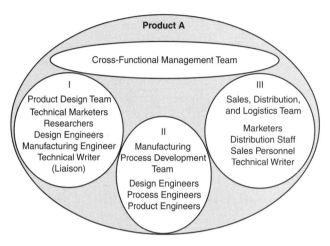

A possible team configuration for the new product development process

---

The question of context and scale

Context and scale are important when you're designing teams. The NPD example illustrates a solution for a relatively complex process within a larger organization. What does that larger organization look like?

A straightforward way to structure an organization is to divide it into units oriented to customer segments or to products or services. Each unit performs a whole process of creation and delivery.

The larger organization might be divided into business units, each of which is a product organization such as the one shown here. Or it might organize itself into business units based on clearly identifiable customer groups.

If the task is small enough, one team might be able to do the whole process. So the unit will be a single team. For example, one team might carry out all the processes to deliver service to the educational market.

It's when the process is complex, with many players—as shown in the NPD example —that you need to create multiple teams for the subprocesses.

The organization may be structured into product-oriented units...

Product A

Product B

Product C

...or customer-oriented units

Consumer Market

Business Market

Educational Market

EXAMPLE: REGIONAL FIELD-OFFICE
TEAMS IN THE INSURANCE INDUSTRY

The insurance company began its design by using a process-mapping technique like the one used for NPD in the previous example. Unlike NPD, which had one major process to be mapped, the insurance company had to map several subprocesses.

❑ Writing new business

❑ Processing claims

❑ Renewing business

❑ Discontinuing business

❑ Etc.

Each subprocess map revealed a different set of flows and interdependencies among the skill sets:

❑ Business planning

❑ Claims processing

❑ Underwriting

❑ Servicing

❑ Marketing

Depending on the day-to-day situation, different combinations of these subprocesses and their interdependencies are necessary and must be balanced with each other. As a result the company decided to incorporate all these skill sets within a team.

This company created teams for customer segments (nonprofit firms, natural-resource firms, general commercial firms). These teams have responsibility for building a profitable business in their segment and servicing it. The teams vary in size, depending on the size of the segment.

Each team has all the skills required to carry out the multiple subprocesses that are required to build and service the business. Each team works out its own work allocation and assignments depending on its mix of activities and competencies.

People are cross-trained in multiple skills, although claims and underwriting require extensive specialized training and are carried out by a subset of team members. Each team has a cross-training plan.

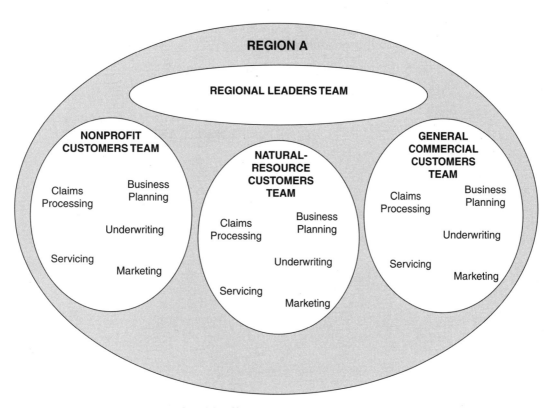

Insurance Company: Regional Field Office

DEFINING WORK TEAMS: WHAT TO DO

To start, remind yourself of (1) the mission, (2) the products and services, and (3) the general skills required in this organization.

If you can visualize the right team structure immediately, draw it on page 2-12.

1 YOUR ORGANIZATION'S MISSION STATEMENT	2 PRODUCTS AND SERVICES
	❏
	❏
	❏
	❏
	❏

3 SKILL SETS

General Skill Sets

(4) Draw a high-level process map of the work for the organization, listing the major tasks. Draw arrows to represent one-way and two-way workflows.

(5) Then circle clusters of tasks that show high task and decision interdependencies.

The most reliable linkages require the most resources.

It's a creative process.

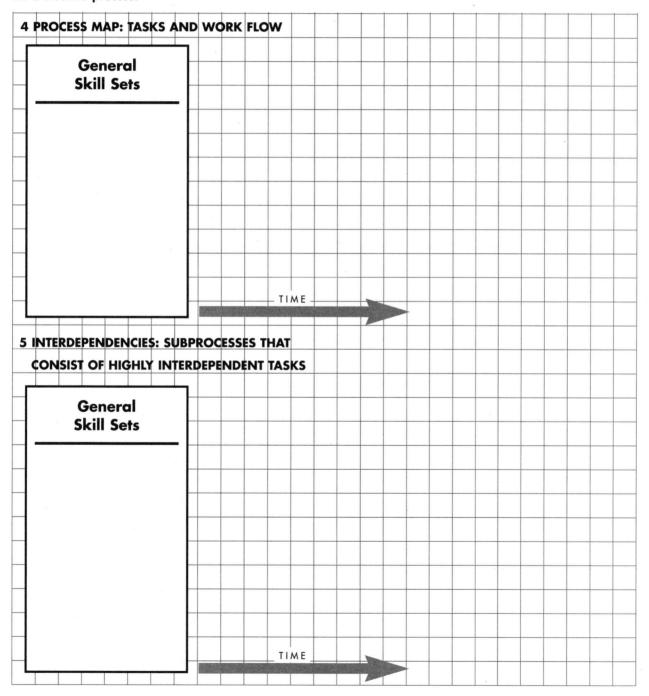

(6) Construct teams to carry out the work of the organization. You may be able to put the entire work process in one team for each product or customer.

OR

If the whole process is too large, form teams to carry out subprocesses that constitute a whole piece of work.

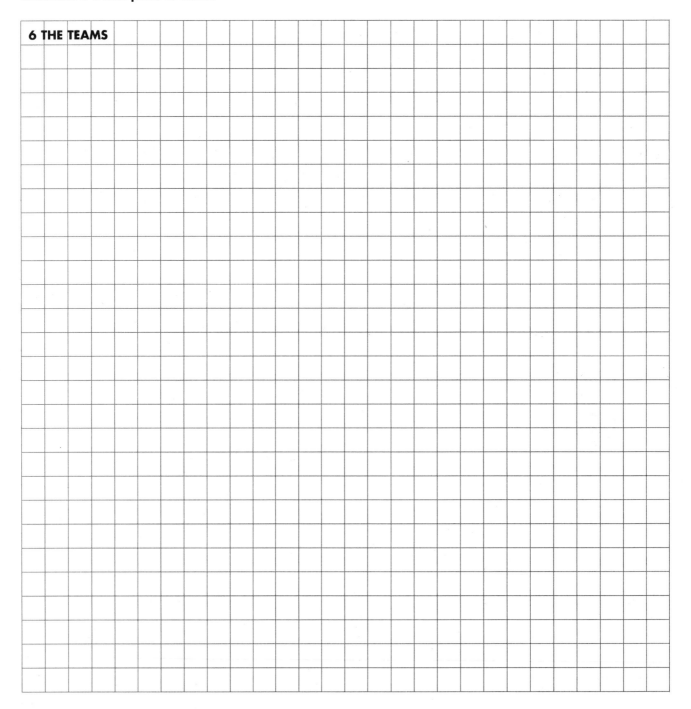

6 THE TEAMS

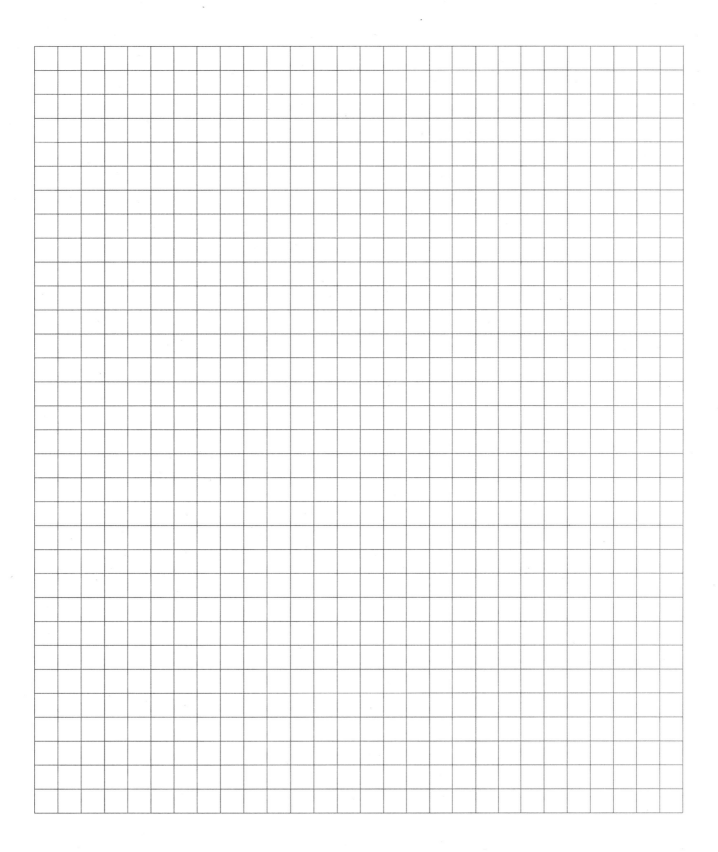

ORGANIZING SCARCE EXPERTISE AND SUPPORT

TWO SPECIAL SITUATIONS

Two types of competencies may require special treatment in a team-based organization:

❑ Technical experts with deep and/or scarce knowledge bases may be in too short supply to dedicate to every team. Or a team may not be able to use such an expert full time.

❑ Support people who perform such work as quality, analytical, finance, and maintenance functions may be needed by a team —but not be needed on a full-time basis.

A team-based organization can allocate these competencies in three ways: dedicated team memberships, multiple team memberships, and shared service groups.

DEDICATED MEMBERS

A team can be more fully self-contained if people with all the required skills become members of the team.

For example, you can place support people in teams or cross-train other team members to carry out these functions.

If the team doesn't need a full-time support person, you can cross-train people who used to be in support roles to perform other tasks needed by the team. Then they can become dedicated team members.

These options don't work as well for scarce technical experts with deep knowledge bases. They may continue to be shared by multiple teams.

MULTIPLE MEMBERSHIPS

If dedicated membership doesn't work, multiple team membership is a possibility. However, multiple team membership can lead to several problems:

❑ Conflicting priorities when multiple teams place demands on the team member

❑ Loss of work time when a team member has to spend time in meetings for multiple teams

❑ Feelings of full-time team members that individuals with split membership aren't committed to the team's success

If multiple team memberships are unavoidable, teams have to explicitly discuss the situation and develop ways to facilitate the integration of such members into the work of the team. Teams also have to set realistic goals with their part-time members for what they can contribute and when.

SHARED SERVICE GROUPS

Shared service groups support work teams:

❑ They may consist of interdependent members who, as a team, carry out a complex process to provide service to the operating teams.

❑ They may be work groups consisting of people who perform their work largely as individuals and whose work is not interdependent.

Technical experts, for example, may work as individuals or as a team to provide consulting or contract services to the work teams. They may go through periods of intense activity supporting a work team. During that period, they may attend work team meetings and be fully integrated with the team's workflow. They may even co-locate during a period of intense involvement. But the work team doesn't expect them to attend all meetings during periods when the team doesn't need their expertise.

Guidelines for allocating special services

If the skill is scarce and not easily cross-trained:

❑ Make the experts members of up to three teams, and create clear agreements among teams about the shared use of this expertise, or

❑ Locate the experts and specialists in a shared service group and have them develop service agreements (sometimes called service contracts) with each. Set up a mechanism to account for team use of shared services.

If the skill is widely held but no team has need for a full-time person with that skill:

❑ Place a specialist in each team and cross-train him or her in other skills needed by the team.

If the skill is relatively easily cross-trained but in short supply:

❑ Place the specialists in a small shared service group and use them to cross-train team members in their skills and to provide consulting help during the learning process.

```
          ┌──────────────────────┐
          │    Actuarial and     │
          │   Business-Analysis  │
          │   Shared Service Group │
          └──────────────────────┘

 ╭──────────╮  ╭──────────╮  ╭──────────╮  ╭──────────╮
 │Customer Team│ │Customer Team│ │Customer Team│ │Customer Team│  . . . etc.
 │ Industry A │ │ Industry B │ │ Industry C │ │ Industry D │
 ╰──────────╯  ╰──────────╯  ╰──────────╯  ╰──────────╯
```

A shared service work group for an insurance field office

The actuarial and business-analysis shared service group:

❑ Consists of three individuals with actuarial and business-analysis skills

❑ Provides support to customer-based teams in analyzing business profitability and in financial and business planning

What to avoid

Don't put resource people and specialized people in a group and call it a team just because you want everyone to be in a team. If people don't have a shared goal and they aren't interdependent, they'll waste a lot of time trying to become a good team. That time would be better spent supporting the work teams.

Conditions for success of shared services

Shared services exist to support the work teams, but their time is not a free commodity. For shared services to work effectively, the organization needs:

❑ A contracting process for the teams to define the services they are going to need—how much, when, and to what specifications

❑ A way to account for the costs of the shared services used by a work team so that the work team uses these services effectively

❑ A goal-setting process to make sure multiple teams aren't counting on using the same resources at the same time

❑ Norms of information sharing and an infrastructure to make it easy for specialists to keep up with team activities

EXAMPLE:
SUPPORT RESOURCES AND SCARCE EXPERTISE
FOR A FOUR-COMPONENT PRODUCT DEVELOPMENT PROJECT

1   ANALYZING AND ASSIGNING RESOURCES

Which skills are needed?	How much does each team need?	Are there enough people with the skills to place in each team?	Can others be cross-trained in this skill?	Solution that keeps teams self-contained or gives them access to skills as needed
Quality	About half time	Yes, two teams each	Yes	Give them multiple team membership, with two teams each. They could train others and pick up additional skills needed by teams so that eventually each team has a person who is half-time quality and half-time something else, with no multiple team memberships.
Test and reliability engineering	Varies from one-quarter to half time Varies during stages of project	No, would require membership in four teams each	Not quickly	Place them in shared service group with clear service contracts with each work team. They meet with work teams during periods of heavy involvement.
Systems engineering (This is an example of a widely held skill.)	About one-third to half time	Yes, one team each	Not easily, but those who have this skill have strong engineering backgrounds	Place them in work teams, with one team each. If necessary, cross-train them in specific engineering skills needed by team or in quality.

2 STRUCTURING SPECIALIZED SUPPORT

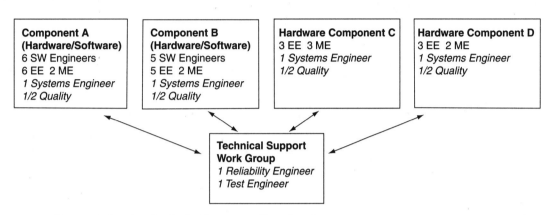

Note: This organization is designing a product that is a system composed of four component subsystems.

3 CREATING A CONTRACT

Here are samples of the kinds of terms that might be part of the contract between the technical support group and the work team.

❏ The test engineer will work with a subteam and provide preliminary test architecture by March 30. From June to December, the engineer will attend team meetings and support prototype testing needs.
   Note: You can provide more exact specifications and additional milestones and due dates.

❏ Team agrees to provide a written assessment of the support person's work at the end of each engagement.

ORGANIZING SCARCE EXPERTISE AND SUPPORT:
WHAT TO DO

Use this matrix to identify and analyze expert and support functions you need in your work teams.

Then develop a plan for allocating skills to teams or work groups.

1 ANALYZE AND ASSIGN RESOURCES

Which skills are needed?	How much does each team need?	Are there enough people with the skills to place in each team?	Can others be cross-trained in this skill?	Solution that keeps teams self-contained or gives them access to skills as needed

© Jossey-Bass, Inc.

2 | STRUCTURE SPECIALIZED SUPPORT

Show the team and/or work-group structure for the support groups, showing interdependencies.

3 | CREATE A CONTRACT TEMPLATE

List the general terms of the contract for each major type of shared resource.

DESIGNING CROSS-TEAM LINKAGES

WHY DO YOU NEED CROSS-TEAM LINKAGES?

It is usually impossible to fully self-contain teams. Many subprocesses require their own teams, but the teams are interdependent.

Unfortunately, once teams have been formed, they have a tendency to become focused on their own activities to the exclusion of the activities of other teams in the organization. They may forget to integrate their work across teams or to share information relevant to other teams.

To prevent the creation of new silos, you need to identify coordination needs and design linkages between teams.

WHEN DO YOU NEED CROSS-TEAM LINKAGES?

Work integration may be informal or formal:

❑ Lots of integration naturally occurs through informal interaction among people whose work is interdependent.

❑ In a traditional, hierarchical organization, formal integration between groups is usually the responsibility of the manager.

❑ In a team-based organization, formal integration is often achieved through lateral linkages.

You need to design lateral linkages when:

❑ Informal integration is not quick enough or reliable enough

❑ You can identify a predictable set of issues that need to be resolved across teams

❑ Teams have an ongoing need for mutual adjustment

TYPES OF LINKAGES

You need to design lateral linkages that meet the needs of the teams. You have several choices:

- ❑ Informal linkages that occur between individuals as needed

- ❑ Electronic linkages such as shared data bases, e-mail, voice mail, and other ways of communicating information to those who need to know

- ❑ Liaisons, who keep apprised of activities of another team and convene appropriate parties when issues arise

- ❑ Overlapping memberships, which enable the work of one team to inform the work of another team

- ❑ Cross-teams, which consist of representatives of interdependent teams and make decisions that integrate the work of the teams they link

Use the least resource-intensive mechanism that reliably integrates the work.

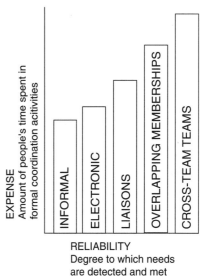

The most reliable linkages require the most resources.

> ### Do you need formal linkages?
>
> The need to have formal linkages may not be apparent to teams at first. But it's important to create expectations for lateral coordination from the very beginning. More experienced teams will be able to determine which kind of linkage will work best for different purposes.

LIAISON ROLES

In this situation, the marketing team has two members, each of whom serves as liaison to one of the product teams. Each product team has a marketing liaison. The functions of the liaisons are

❑ To make the other teams aware of information that's important to them

❑ To be initial contact points for other teams and their own teams

OVERLAPPING MEMBERSHIPS

In the new product development example earlier in this module, three engineers have full membership roles in both the product design team and the manufacturing process development team. The need for the overlapping membership is evident in the process and interdependence analyses described on pages 2-6 and 2-7.

These overlapping members work in both teams and, in so doing, help integrate the two subprocesses.

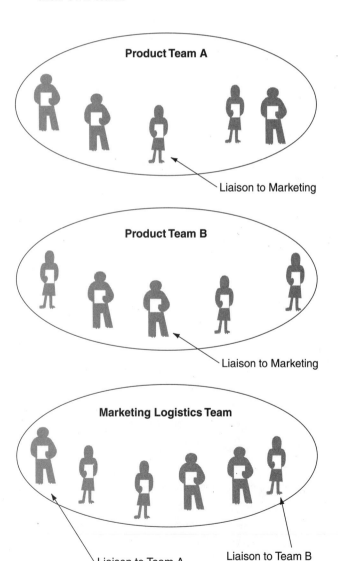

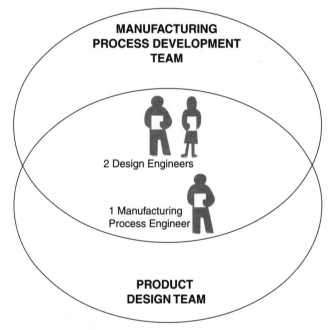

CROSS-TEAM INTEGRATING TEAM

This example is a software integrating team. It links the two component teams developing software in the example shown on page 2-19. It also integrates another software design team housed in an external organization.

Its functions are

❑ To deal with interdependencies when specifications and change order procedures are insufficient —for example, when fundamental aspects of the system, such as its architecture, have to be changed.

❑ To make sure that information is being documented and communicated in a timely manner among the three organizations

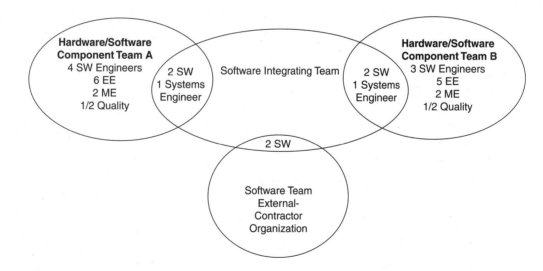

DESIGNING CROSS-TEAM LINKAGES:
WHAT TO DO

Identify the needs for linkages across work teams and design approaches that
ensure the linkages occur.

1 LINKAGE NEEDS	2 THE TEAMS
What issues arise that require resolution across teams?	*Which teams are involved?*
What ongoing work adjustment is required across teams?	

© Jossey-Bass, Inc.

3 | THE SOLUTIONS

Draw the team solutions that provide the best lateral linkages for each need. Use the approach that consumes the least amount of people's time to accomplish integration effectively.

DESIGNING INVOLVEMENT AND IMPROVEMENT TEAMS

INFLUENCING THE CONTEXT

Team members need to influence the context in which they work. So team-based organizations often set up special-purpose teams to

❑ Make decisions and perform tasks that were previously the domain of management

❑ Introduce improvements in the organizational design

These teams typically consist of a representative group of organizational members and perform tasks that affect the whole organization. They may be temporary teams or standing teams.

Using such teams has several advantages:

❑ Decision quality improves as relevant knowledge and perspectives are applied.

❑ Involvement of members contributes to a sense of ownership and commitment to the success of the organization.

❑ Decisions may be seen as less arbitrary and unilateral, particularly if there are clear and well-communicated criteria.

This approach is consistent with a way of managing that encourages the members of the organization to accept responsibility and feel they can influence business success.

INVOLVEMENT TEAMS

In a team-based organization, representative teams are often set up to carry out tasks that were previously done by management, such as:

❑ Assigning people to teams

❑ Coordinating the performance-appraisal process

❑ Determining a training plan

❑ Determining special awards

These **involvement teams** are given the responsibility and authority to perform integrative and management roles in the organization.

Team-based organizations generally have a formal management team that sets direction and allocates resources. This team will be discussed in the next module.

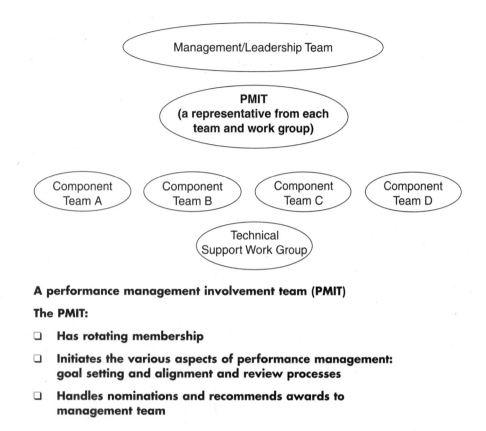

A performance management involvement team (PMIT)

The PMIT:

❑ **Has rotating membership**

❑ **Initiates the various aspects of performance management: goal setting and alignment and review processes**

❑ **Handles nominations and recommends awards to management team**

Success factors for involvement teams

❑ Establishing a clear charter

❑ Assuring representativeness of the people in the organization

❑ Maintaining a close connection to work teams—with well-defined input mechanisms and proven responsiveness

❑ Articulating clear criteria for decision making so decisions are seen as equitable

❑ Rotating members over time and providing widespread opportunities for involvement

IMPROVEMENT TEAMS

Improvement teams address ways to improve the performance of the organization. Some examples are

❏ Quality improvement teams

❏ Process-redesign teams

❏ Problem-solving teams

❏ Teams that generate or implement new approaches, such as new applications of information technology

WHEN TO USE IMPROVEMENT TEAMS

In today's demanding competitive environment, all organizations need to continually improve their capabilities. However, improvement teams consume time and energy of the organization's pool of talent, and managers are often reluctant to focus people's energies on making improvements. Managers must decide how much improvement activity can and should be sustained.

Improvement teams should be set up to:

❏ Address high-leverage improvement areas that will improve key performance parameters

❏ Manage the planning and implementation of changes to process and method that the organization is being asked to implement by higher levels of the firm

Improvement teams should be set up **only** if managers are willing to dedicate time and resources to making the team successful:

❏ For quicker leverage, dedicate a small group to an intense effort.

❏ For longer-term efforts, part-time teams can be successful.

If people aren't dedicated to the effort, the total person-hours will be greater because split priorities create inefficiency.

Selection tips for involvement and improvement teams

❏ Broaden involvement to give influence and growth opportunities to many members.

❏ Don't limit involvement to a chosen few.

❏ Involve the teams in selection of their representatives to involvement teams.

❏ For improvement teams, make sure that all necessary knowledge bases are included.

Regional
Leaders Team

**Groupware-Implementation
Improvement Team
(a representative from each
customer-segment team and
other groups)**

Actuarial and Business-Analysis Shared Service Group

Customer Team
Industry A

Customer Team
Industry B

Customer Team
Industry C

Customer Team
Industry D

A system-upgrade improvement team

The Groupware-Implementation Improvement Team:

❑ **Plans and manages system installation and training**

❑ **Holds sessions to discuss uses and benefits**

❑ **Manages a "lessons learned" sharing process**

Success factors for improvement teams

❑ Clearly linking improvement teams to the strategy of the organization

❑ Creating only as many improvement teams as staffing levels allow

❑ Budgeting time, with as much member time as possible dedicated to the team

❑ Treating the work of the team as a project that is managed

❑ Building the work of the team into performance objectives for the organization

❑ Defining a clear charter

❑ Establishing an information and input link to the work teams that will be affected by changes

❑ Building in clear authority and support from management

❑ Including participation in these teams in individuals' performance reviews

DESIGNING INVOLVEMENT AND IMPROVEMENT TEAMS: WHAT TO DO

Think through the arenas in which *important* organizational approaches and decisions can be made by a representative group of organizational members. Pick the high-payoff decisions—ones that matter to people and are perceived as arbitrary when made unilaterally by management.

❑ **INVOLVEMENT TEAMS**	
What are the important arenas of decision making where an involvement team could be set up to contribute to members' stake in the organization?	
❑ **CHARTER FOR TOP-PRIORITY INVOLVEMENT TEAMS**	
Team:	*Team:*
Charter Elements:	*Charter Elements:*
Membership Composition:	*Membership Composition:*

© Jossey-Bass, Inc.

❏ **IMPROVEMENT TEAMS**	
What are the important arenas where a performance-improvement team could make a difference?	
❏ **CHARTER FOR TOP-** **PRIORITY PROJECTS**	
Project:	Project:
Charter Elements:	Charter Elements:
Membership Composition:	Membership Composition:

WHAT'S NEXT

In this module, you've done the hard work of analyzing your organization's team needs, including

❑ The appropriate work teams for your organization

❑ The best treatment of shared resources

❑ The linkage requirements between teams and across teams

❑ Arenas in which organizational members can become more involved in decision making and resource allocation

❑ Key improvement projects

You'll need to communicate the results of this analysis to your organization—and gather feedback.

All teams need a complete charter. Module 8 will provide a generic approach to chartering teams. Chartering is an important early step in implementing a team-based organization —but you need a framework for your team-based organization before you formulate charters.

You'll need to begin by building a leadership framework for your team-based organization. The next module will help you build this framework.

You are not finished with design

The structures you have just designed must now be augmented by designing processes and systems to support them.

Your team designs will naturally go through a process of revision as you present them to the organization and get feedback. Give yourself time to think about the structure you've designed, get lots of input, and expect to make changes.

TO DO

DESIGNING MANAGEMENT AND LEADERSHIP ROLES

ACTIVITIES IN THIS MODULE

DESIGNING
LEADERSHIP INTO TEAMS

COMPOSING THE
MANAGEMENT TEAM

A team-based organization is not leaderless—quite the contrary. In a team-based organization, lots of people and teams play leadership roles. Many of the leaders are not managers.

In a multiple-team organization, leadership is required within each team. Also, systemwide leadership is necessary to integrate the organization:

❑ To establish overall direction

❑ To make sure that different parts of the organization are working together

❑ To create the context in which teams perform

This module helps you design leadership roles and relationships within teams and across the organization.

LEADERSHIP IN TEAM-BASED ORGANIZATIONS

LEADERSHIP IS A SET OF ROLES AND ACTIVITIES

A number of leadership functions are needed in a team-based organization:

- ❑ Direction setting
- ❑ Decision making
- ❑ Administration functions
- ❑ Work coordination
- ❑ Team process leadership and facilitation
- ❑ Management of team boundaries
- ❑ Technical mentoring
- ❑ Team capability development
- ❑ Introduction of improvements
- ❑ Performance management

Each of these functions is necessary for the team to be successful in accomplishing its mission and improving its performance through time. Even when teams are self-managing, a team-based organization needs to define approaches for accomplishing these tasks.

APPROACHES TO LEADERSHIP

Leadership roles may be

- ❑ Formal or informal
- ❑ Hierarchical or nonhierarchical (performed by peers)
- ❑ Permanent, temporary, or even rotating

Much leadership emerges informally. However, the more complex and dynamic the work, the less the team-based organization can rely on informal leadership. Most team-based organizations have a combination of different kinds of formal and informal leadership roles.

Formal leadership roles are not necessarily hierarchical management positions. They are clear assignments that give particular individuals or teams the legitimacy to perform certain leadership tasks for and within the team and the team-based organization. These assignments can be made by the team itself or by management.

Leadership functions can even be carried out by teams set up for this purpose. The management team is one example. An improvement team is another.

Work may move through different phases, and team leadership may change depending on the critical work activities during a particular phase.

Clarifying leadership roles

Many leadership roles in a team-based organization rely on the exercise of lateral influence. Legitimacy for the exercise of this influence comes from a clarification among all involved of what the leadership role is and how it will operate. This clarification requires discussion with the members of the organization.

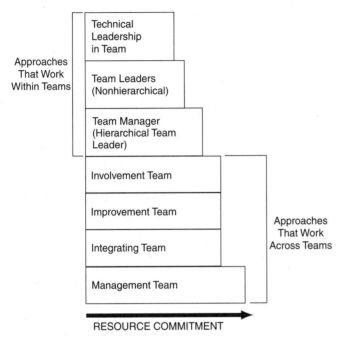

Approaches That Work Within Teams

- Technical Leadership in Team
- Team Leaders (Nonhierarchical)
- Team Manager (Hierarchical Team Leader)
- Involvement Team
- Improvement Team
- Integrating Team
- Management Team

Approaches That Work Across Teams

RESOURCE COMMITMENT

Various approaches to leadership require different amounts of resource commitment.

Formal leadership roles and teams are good ways to build in necessary leadership capacity. Because they represent resource commitment, they should be used only as required for effective lateral and hierarchical integration of the organization.

FUNCTIONAL LEADERSHIP

Most organizations need to foster functional expertise even though they are organized into cross-functional performing units. Each organization needs to design an approach to technical mentoring, improving technical processes, and monitoring and updating technical capabilities.

Functional leaders may lead these activities even though they may not directly manage the technical resources of the organization. They may work by

- ❑ Setting up representative councils or task teams
- ❑ Coaching and using informal influence
- ❑ Official mentoring responsibilities
- ❑ Participating in performance management
- ❑ Auditing technical performance

Functional leaders may be working members of teams with a special assignment to provide technical mentoring within the team.

When discipline expertise is dispersed among teams, the organization needs systems to develop and update those skills. It also needs to ensure that such expertise is explicitly valued by the organization.

Management roles

In this book we use the terms *manager* and *management team* when referring to leadership roles that have formal, hierarchical authority over the organizational unit (e.g., team, project, business) they lead.

DESIGNING LEADERSHIP INTO TEAMS

KEY DESIGN PRINCIPLES

To promote maximum team ownership and account-ability:

❏ Move as much self-management as possible into the team. The more aspects of leadership that are done by a manager, the more team members will rely on their manager and feel responsible only for their subpieces.

❏ Share leadership and self-management responsibilities among team members. Ideally, all members are leaders and feel responsible for performance.

❏ Make sure leadership and management tasks are explicitly assigned. Who does a particular leadership task is less important than the fact that responsibility is explicitly assigned so that the task gets done.

WHAT IS SELF-MANAGEMENT?

Team self-managment is when team members perform many of the management tasks that used to be done by supervisors. There are different approaches to leadership in self-managed teams. One approach does not fit all kinds of work settings.

As teams gain experience, they can take on more self-management. The organization needs a plan to develop self-management skills and encourage teams to accept more responsibility.

A possible configuration for leadership roles in a team

SELECTING LEADERS

Leadership roles are necessary for carrying out the work of the organization.

By performing leadership roles—hierarchical or not—people in the organization develop competencies that make them more valuable to the organization and that increase the overall competency level of the organization.

The organization has a key interest in making sure that its members are getting leadership experience. This experience ensures that

❑ The organization has sufficient leadership capability to function effectively

❑ People are being prepared to assume management roles

An individual team also has an interest in making sure its leadership roles are being performed effectively so it can carry out its mission—and its members have the opportunity to learn and grow by playing different leadership roles.

Leaders can be

❑ Appointed by managers

❑ Selected by the team

❑ Selected by managers and the team working together, perhaps by the managers with input from the team

If the team has some input into who plays various leadership roles, it will be more likely to respond positively to influence attempts from the leader. The most important factor is that there are clear criteria for each leadership position.

THE TEAM IS ACCOUNTABLE

The team is collectively accountable for its performance. Leaders take responsibility for making sure the team attends to some aspects of its own functioning, but it is the team, not the leader alone, that carries out its mission.

❑ Collective accountability is essential in a team-based organization.

If management continues to hold a team leader individually accountable and if management's first instinct in a troubled team is to replace the team leader, the team members may not fully accept their own responsibility and accountability. Furthermore, team leaders will be more likely to assume traditional control-oriented styles because they know they are individually at risk.

When a team is struggling, managers should address the problems first with the team. Team leadership may or may not be the source of the problem.

Inexperienced team leaders need coaching and support in order to become effective.

Leaders are models for the new logic

❑ They coach their teams as they evolve.

❑ They champion the practice of the new logic.

❑ They help people adjust to the new organization.

EXAMPLE:
LEADERSHIP ROLES IN TEAMS

Here's an example of a framework developed by an organization for its leadership roles.

Note: This is just one example of leadership roles. Each organization needs to determine its own leadership requirements and selection approaches.

LEADERSHIP NEEDS	LEADERSHIP ROLES	HOW TO SELECT LEADERS
Work Teams		
Business/project/workload	Team leader	Management team selects with work team input
Team process facilitation	Process leader	Work team selects
Technical integration	Systems integration leader	Systems engineer and management team select
Improvement Teams		
Project leadership	Project leader	Management team selects
Management-team interface	Management-team liaison	Team selects (may be project leader)
Involvement Teams		
Team leadership	Team leader	Team selects
Software Integrating Team		
Technical leadership	Emergent, informal	Not applicable
Management-team interface	Team leader	Team selects

DESIGNING LEADERSHIP INTO TEAMS:
WHAT TO DO

Identify the leadership needs and roles in each of the teams you created in
Module 2 and think about the best ways to select the people to fill those roles.

LEADERSHIP NEEDS FOR EACH TYPE OF TEAM	LEADERSHIP ROLES	HOW TO SELECT LEADERS

COMPOSING THE MANAGEMENT TEAM

SYSTEMWIDE MANAGEMENT

Module 2 described several of the mechanisms for systemwide leadership: integrating teams, involvement teams, and improvement teams are all "leaders." So are people in cross-team work-facilitation roles. Their work helps set the stage for effective performance in the team-based organization.

In addition, a team-based organization needs a **management team** whose main purpose is to provide systemwide leadership. Such teams might exist at multiple levels:

❑ A division might have multiple business units. The division-level management team provides leadership across the whole division.

❑ Each business unit might comprise multiple teams. The business-unit management team provides leadership across the teams.

WHAT IS A MANAGEMENT TEAM?

The management team for the organization includes a general manager and other members who represent different perspectives, knowledge bases, and/or teams within the organization.

The **general manager** at the business-unit level may be a program manager, regional manager, or product-line manager who is responsible for a multiple-team subunit.

Other members of management teams may be managers, but they need not be. They may be leaders from the various teams or representatives of the different functions represented within the teams.

FUNCTIONS OF THE MANAGEMENT TEAM

The function of the management team is to:

❑ Set direction

❑ Make authoritative resource allocation decisions

❑ Make decisions that involve the whole organization

❑ Monitor performance and initiate performance-improvement approaches

❑ Make sure that the organization is designed for optimal performance of its mission

❑ Model teaming norms, coach, and reinforce teaming

❑ Make sure the learning processes to develop effective teaming are in place

Management teams can carry out their roles in a participative style. Their members represent the various perspectives and teams (performing units) of the organization. In addition, they can regularly solicit input from team members, open their meetings to other organizational members, and delegate some organization-wide leadership to involvement teams.

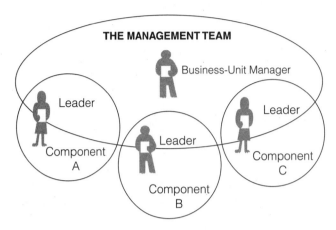

A leadership team composed of team leaders

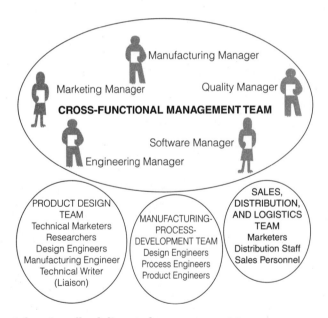

A functionally delineated management team

EXAMPLE:
A MODEL FOR SELECTING MANAGEMENT TEAM MEMBERS

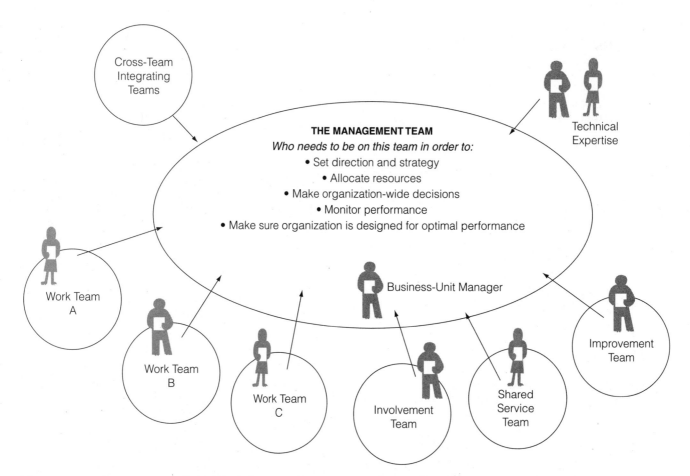

THE MANAGEMENT TEAM

Who needs to be on this team in order to:

- Set direction and strategy
- Allocate resources
- Make organization-wide decisions
- Monitor performance
- Make sure organization is designed for optimal performance

Cross-Team Integrating Teams

Technical Expertise

Work Team A

Work Team B

Work Team C

Business-Unit Manager

Involvement Team

Shared Service Team

Improvement Team

The management team needs to have the necessary perspectives to do its job well. One approach, illustrated here, is to include someone from every team in the organization. Your organization may require a different approach.

In general, smaller teams are better able to make decisions efficiently. The goal is to maintain a manageable size while establishing systematic ways to get regular input from all teams.

COMPOSING THE MANAGEMENT TEAM:
WHAT TO DO

Determine the composition of your management team. Some questions to ask are: Does the management team need representatives from each team? Who else needs to be on the team?

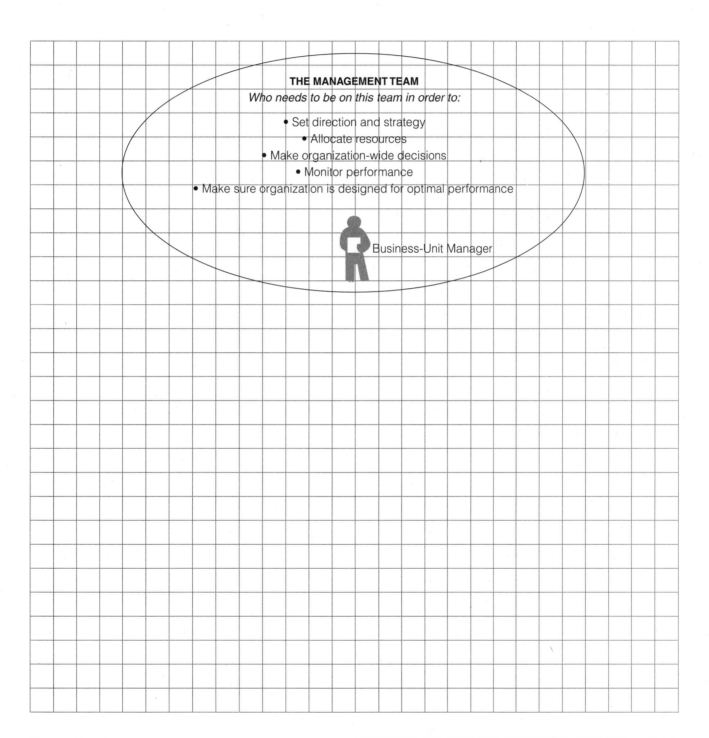

THE MANAGEMENT TEAM

Who needs to be on this team in order to:

- Set direction and strategy
- Allocate resources
- Make organization-wide decisions
- Monitor performance
- Make sure organization is designed for optimal performance

Business-Unit Manager

WHAT'S NEXT

In this module, you've designed the formal leadership of your organization. You've identified the approaches you need to deal effectively and efficiently with the complexity in your organization. You need to discuss this leadership plan with the members of the organization.

You also need to select individuals to fill the roles you've designed. Selection of leaders is the most important but also the most contentious decision made in an organization:

❑ You need a plan that assures that interested and qualified people have an opportunity to get leadership experience and develop leadership skills.

❑ You need a plan to help them gain the new skills and perspectives they need to lead teams.

With your team design and your leadership plan, you have the structural skeleton of your organization in place. Now it's time to turn to the processes that will allow your structure to work.

TO DO

© Jossey-Bass, Inc.

SETTING DIRECTION ACROSS THE ORGANIZATION

ACTIVITY IN THIS MODULE

CREATING A FRAMEWORK
FOR DIRECTION SETTING

The various parts of the team-based organization need to be moving in a coordinated fashion. The direction-setting processes are part of the glue that makes this coordinated action possible.

In a team-based organization, everyone shares the goals of the whole. The goal-setting process creates ownership and awareness, and a clear strategy provides a context for decision making.

Goals need to be continuously aligned, communicated, and updated as circumstances change. This module outlines a framework for these tasks.

PRINCIPLES OF DIRECTION SETTING

CLEAR DIRECTION ENABLES LATERAL DECISION MAKING

Team-based organizations rely on clear direction and broadly held knowledge of that direction. Team decisions across functions and interteam decisions often entail complex and contentious trade-offs. These are facilitated by a commonly held understanding of organizational direction.

Teams are more effective if people know

❑ Where the organization is headed

❑ Its strategy

❑ Its priorities and goals

❑ Success criteria

❑ Its plans

SETTING DIRECTION IS A TWO-WAY PROCESS

Responsibility for setting overall organizational direction lies with the management team.

But work teams often have knowledge that's relevant to the development of strategy, plans, and goals. They may have pertinent knowledge about

❑ Customers

❑ Technical issues

❑ Organizational needs and resources

Commitment to direction is more likely if the work teams feel their perspectives have been taken into account.

EVERYONE SHARES THE GOALS OF THE UNIT

This principle provides the impetus to integrate laterally. Individuals and teams don't become narrowly focused on their piece—out of context—if they are owners of their own goals and the goals of the larger unit.

"It's not my job" doesn't make sense if everyone shares the team and organization goals.

DIRECTION IS EMPOWERING

Providing direction is not the same as being directive.

Being directive is telling the teams what to do and how to do it. It's carefully monitoring and often overriding the work of the team. This is disempowering.

The direction that's important in a team-based organization is the kind that provides a framework for decision making. Within that framework, organizational members can be empowered to make decisions within and across teams.

Decisions and direction

Teams will be making trade-off decisions that require a knowledge of organizational strategy and direction.

CREATING A FRAMEWORK FOR DIRECTION SETTING

ALIGNING THE ORGANIZATION

The goal-setting process provides a framework that aligns the various parts of the organization. It should include:

❑ The alignment of goals across levels. Team goals should be aligned with business-unit goals. Individual goals should be aligned with team goals.

❑ The alignment of goals laterally. The work of different teams has to fit together to achieve the business-unit goals. The work of different team members has to fit together to achieve the team's goals.

❑ The alignment of the goals of shared services with the goals of the work teams.

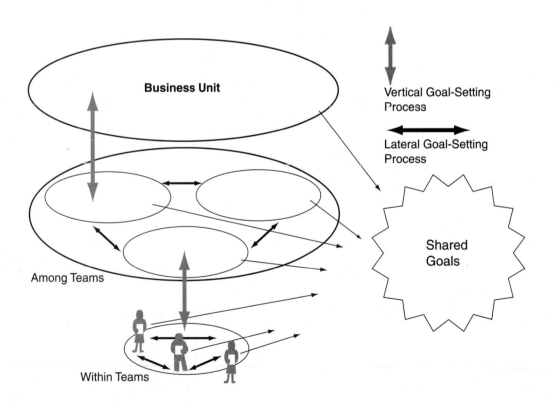

© Jossey-Bass, Inc.

GETTING EVERYONE INVOLVED

Involvement in planning and goal setting is imperative.

In the traditional organization, managers develop and "keep" the plan. In a team-based organization, the plan has to be owned by everyone, and everyone is accountable.

Planning is a collective process that enables:

❑ Input from team members

❑ Negotiation and adjustment across levels and teams

❑ An understanding by all members of the rationale behind the goals

❑ An understanding of how the goals of the various parts of the organization fit together

BUILDING IN CHANGE

Plans need to be living documents.

Aligned plans are part of a glue that enables integrated action. But as conditions change, plans must also change. There needs to be a process for updating plans and making sure that everyone is informed:

❑ As the organization carries out its work and teams make day-to-day decisions, strategic direction and plans need to be readily accessible to everyone in a usable format.

❑ As direction changes, the changes must be documented and disseminated.

Computer-based information networks can be ideal mechanisms for achieving both the availability and flexibility demanded.

EXAMPLE:
A FRAMEWORK FOR SETTING SHARED GOALS AND PLANS

THE BUSINESS UNIT

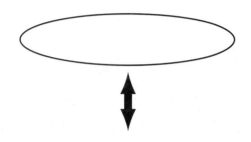

WHAT: *Business-unit goals and plans*

WHO: *Management team*

HOW: *Consensually, starting with input from teams and support units and with the strategy and plans of the larger organization*

WHEN: *Yearly, but revisited quarterly or as needed*

ACROSS TEAMS

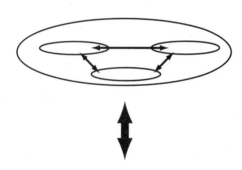

WHAT: *Alignment of goals and plans among teams and support units*

WHO: *Representatives and/or leaders from teams and support units*

HOW: *Meeting as an integration team to align team/unit plans in light of the business plan*

WHEN: *Following planning at the business-unit level*

TEAM AND TEAM MEMBERS

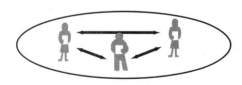

WHAT: *Team or support-unit goals and plans and alignment of member goals and plans*

WHO: *Team or support unit members*

HOW: *Meeting as a team or support unit*

WHEN: *Team first provides input to business planning and then team plans are finalized based on business-unit plans and interteam needs.*

CREATING A FRAMEWORK FOR DIRECTION SETTING: WHAT TO DO

Think about the kinds of plans your organization needs at each level—and who should be involved. Consider different ways to create the plans, including computer-based participatory planning methods.

THE BUSINESS UNIT

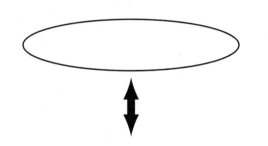

ACROSS TEAMS

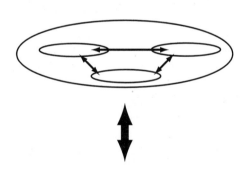

TEAM AND TEAM MEMBERS

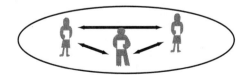

WHAT:	
WHO:	
HOW:	
WHEN:	
WHAT:	
WHO:	
HOW:	
WHEN:	
WHAT:	
WHO:	
HOW:	
WHEN:	

WHAT'S NEXT

In this module, you've identified the key elements of direction setting in your team-based organization.

❑ You'll need to build these elements into your organization by establishing practices for developing, sharing, and updating strategies, goals, and plans—in such a manner that people are knowedgeable and can contribute effectively.

Direction setting is one of the key ongoing processes in a team-based organization. The next two modules address two others: decision making and communication.

TO DO

BUILDING A FRAMEWORK FOR DECISION MAKING

In a team-based organization, decision making is shared laterally.

Clarity of responsibility and authority is critical to doing effective work laterally. Responsibility often can't be neatly partitioned. It's important to know when decisions have to be made jointly—and to identify everyone who needs input.

Decisions may also be made in a variety of different ways. It's important for a lateral organization to have clearly stated decision-making norms—and practices that support those norms.

This module provides a framework for allocation of responsibility and decision-making authority in a team-based organization—as well as principles to guide the development of decision-making norms.

CHARTING RESPONSIBILITY AND AUTHORITY

RESPONSIBILITY AND AUTHORITY ARE KEY

Team-based organizations place task responsibility and decision-making authority in appropriately composed teams. Many decisions and responsibilities that were previously the domain of the management hierarchy are moved into lateral structures.

To avoid confusion, ambiguity, and delays, responsibility and authority must be clearly delineated and communicated. People need to know what authority and responsibility they have and where various decisions get made.

Authority often can't be neatly packaged:

❑ Teams can make some decisions only with information and input from others.

❑ Teams may make decisions that involve organizational resources and may need approval from the management team.

❑ Multiple teams may have to make a decision jointly.

THE SCOPE OF DECISION MAKING

Different teams have different decision-making content and scope.

Work teams can make decisions within their domain of responsibility. However, if their decisions will constrain other teams, they may need to make those decisions with the other teams. At a minimum, the interdependent teams need rapid notification.

Integrating teams, involvement teams, and improvement teams make decisions with a broader scope—across teams and across the organization. Their decisions define context and provide direction for the work teams. Their authority is defined in their charter, but their legitimacy in the eyes of the organization depends on

❑ Their responsiveness to the needs of the units doing the work that delivers service and product

❑ Their alignment with the strategy of the organization

The **management team** makes authoritative strategy and resource allocation decisions for the unit as a whole. It also has the ultimate authority to resolve issues in the organization.

ESCALATION PATHS

Sometimes a team can't make a decision even though it has the authority to make it. It may require a broader perspective than the team members have. The team members may not be able to agree on the priorities and make the necessary trade-offs. Or the team may not have the experience to know how to make the decision.

To prevent gridlock and also to increase decision quality, the team may have to escalate the decision—to get the management team or other leadership teams involved in making it.

Escalating the decision doesn't mean giving up ownership. The management team may

❑ Make the decision jointly with the team that has escalated it

❑ Give input to the team

❑ Teach the team how to make the decision

❑ Make decisions that clarify the situation for the team

Streamlining decision making

Organizations often move to teams to achieve speed—and then become concerned when their teams take longer to make decisions.

Cross-functional teams may take longer to make decisions. But that time often more than pays for itself because people understand, support, and faithfully execute the decision—and the execution is faster.

Decision making itself will be faster if:

❑ Responsibility is clear

❑ Goals and priorities are clear

❑ Teams have an effective process

❑ There is a clear escalation path for decisions that the team can't resolve

---

EXAMPLE:
A DECISION-MAKING RESPONSIBILITY AND AUTHORITY CHART

WHAT THIS SAMPLE CHART SHOWS

A good way to communicate the decision-making responsibility and authority framework for the organization is through a responsibility chart. It shows:

D   Who has authority to decide

R   Who has the responsibility to recommend

I   Whose input needs to be considered

N   Who needs to be informed

U   Who is uninvolved

	Changes to Specifications	Software/ Hardware Trade-offs	Technical Design	Individual Design Task Assignments
Management Team	D	I	N, I	N
Functional Mentors	I	U	N, I	N
Design Team	I, R	D	D (within component)	D
Software Integrating Team	N	I	D (interface decisions)	U
Systems Integrating Team	I, R	I, R	D (systemwide fit issues)	U
Escalation Path		Design team to management team	Design team to integrating teams	To functional bosses

CHARTING DECISION-MAKING RESPONSIBILITY AND AUTHORITY: WHAT TO DO

Create your own decision-making responsibility chart in this grid. List key decision areas across the top of the chart. List teams—and individuals with particular authority—down the left. Fill in the boxes with the levels of responsibility and authority that are appropriate in your organization.

D Who has authority to decide

R Who has the responsibility to recommend

I Whose input needs to be considered

N Who needs to be informed

U Who is uninvolved

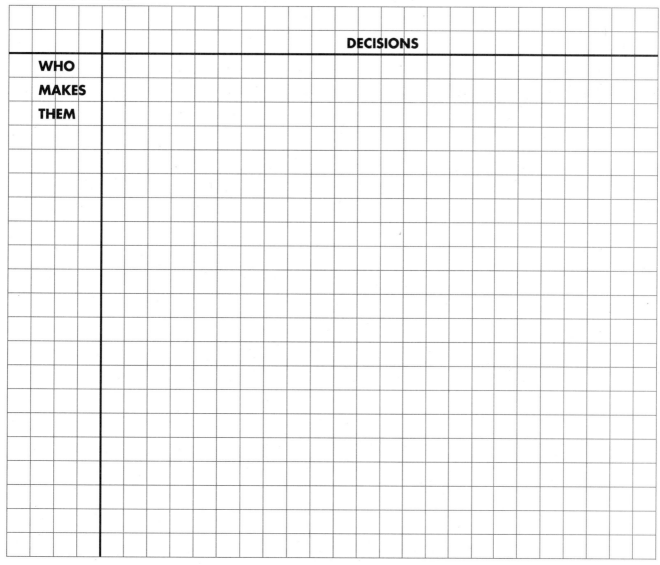

DECISIONS

WHO
MAKES
THEM

DRAFTING NORMS FOR DECISION MAKING

DECISION BY CONSENSUS

For decisions that affect the whole team and that need to be based on the perspectives of all members, team **consensus** is desirable. Such decisions include:

❑ Procedural decisions such as "How are we going to operate as a team?"

❑ Plans that require coordinated action

❑ Some technical decisions that require trade-offs and optimization, taking into account the varying knowledge bases of several individuals

In these situations, consensus will lead to greater ownership and more uniform implementation.

OTHER DECISION MODES

Teams need several decision modes. In addition to consensus:

❑ Experts in the team may make decisions in their domain of expertise, after getting input from other members who have relevant information.

❑ A subgroup of the team may make decisions that don't require time and input from others.

❑ The team can delegate to a team member decisions that don't need to be based on multiple perspectives.

❑ Teams can vote if the decision is based primarily on preference.

Decision making will be faster and most effective if teams use the decision-making mode that's most appropriate. Decisions become "unmade" if appropriate parties are not involved. They take longer if the team involves people unnecessarily or seeks unnecessary consensus on every issue.

Special issues of cross-functional decision making

Members from different functions often bring different knowledge bases, algorithms, styles, priorities, viewpoints, and values. Cross-functional decision making depends on effective processes for surfacing these differences and for creating some understanding of each other's frame of reference.

Effective cross-functional teams systematically consider others' intellectual contributions and points of view, and search for solutions and decisions that build on the whole set of expertise and experience available to them.

SYSTEMATIC DECISION PROCESSES

Decision making is quicker and more effective if teams use systematic processes.

Systematic processes specify the way certain decisions will be made, including steps to be followed, data to be considered, and parties to be included. Examples of systematic processes are:

❏ Multistep TQM processes

❏ Trade-off study formats

❏ Steps for make-buy analyses

The use of systematic processes leads to shared understanding of how decisions are made, which facilitates collaboration among diverse participants. It also leads to greater agreement about the decision.

When applied across the organization, systematic processes serve as a glue that enables people to work together across teams and to move between teams.

A NEW SET OF NORMS

Norms are the patterns of behavior that are accepted and expected in a group. Team-based organizations have to develop norms of:

❏ Actively listening to one another and discussing one another's perspectives

❏ Following systematic processes for decision making

❏ Including all relevant parties

❏ Surfacing all relevant information and different perspectives

❏ Working toward agreement rather than tenaciously protecting one's own viewpoint

❏ Acknowledging and utilizing expertise

❏ Supporting and implementing team decisions

It helps to have an explicitly stated set of values about how the organization will make decisions that provide the foundation for behavioral norms.

Managers and leaders set the tone for decision making

An organization's managers and leaders set the tone for effective lateral decision making by:

❏ Providing training, facilitation, and coaching

❏ Modeling team decision-making norms and practices

❏ Stressing the importance of appropriate input and collaboration

❏ Intervening in team decision making only when necessary

It may be necessary for a manager to intervene in order to appropriately frame a decision from an organizational standpoint or to get a team to reconsider a bad decision. Managers should not intervene just because they prefer a different course of action.

DRAFTING DECISION-MAKING NORMS:
WHAT TO DO

Create a draft list of the decision-making norms that you feel need to guide
decision making in your organization. Then identify practices that support those
values.

NORMS	
An example of a norm:	
❑ Surface and consider all knowledge and perspectives when making a team decision	
❑	❑
❑	❑
❑	❑
❑	❑
❑	❑
❑	❑

PRACTICES	
An example of a practice:	
❑ Flip-chart all relevant perspectives about hardware/software trade-offs, giving each person a chance to contribute before beginning a cost-benefit analysis.	
❑	❑
❑	❑
❑	❑
❑	❑
❑	❑
❑	❑

✓ WHAT'S NEXT

You've created two documents that need to be part of the shared understanding of members of the organization: a responsibility chart and a list of decision-making norms and practices.

❑ You'll need to share these documents, get input, and make them living documents that describe the way the organization operates.

In the next module, you'll create a framework for communicating across the organization.

TO DO

MODULE

CREATING A FRAMEWORK FOR COMMUNICATION

ACTIVITY IN THIS MODULE

DRAFTING A NEW
COMMUNICATION
STRATEGY

An effective communication framework for team-based organization provides a foundation for lateral work. It doesn't require a manager to be central to the conduct of work.

The aim is to make information readily and efficiently available to everyone but not to inundate people with unnecessary information. People must be clearly responsible for sharing information others need and for accessing information they themselves need.

Knowledge about the big picture and about performance is essential if members of the team-based organization are going to feel responsibility for team and organization performance and to make good decisions from an organization perspective.

This module presents some of these key concepts about communication in a team-based organization and helps you think through a strategy for your own organization.

© Jossey-Bass, Inc.

6-1

INFORMATION NEEDS IN A TEAM-BASED ORGANIZATION

INFORMATION IS WIDELY DISTRIBUTED

In the team-based organization, work is performed and coordinated laterally. Decisions are made laterally too. Widely distributed information is the enabler of team decision making and coordination. Communication cannot be narrowly targeted and focused.

Information must be broadly held and available throughout the organization, including information about

❑ The big picture—so that people have an understanding of the system they are part of

❑ What's going on in other functions, departments, and teams—so people can work together effectively

❑ The various parts of the process—so that the whole process can be integrated

INFORMATION FLOWS IN ALL DIRECTIONS

In the traditional organization, information primarily flows vertically. It's the job of management and supervision to share information as needed.

In the team-based organization, information flows in all directions. Each team must

❑ Distribute information

❑ Attend to relevant information from all parts of the organization

Vertical aggregation of data and reporting of information are still critical. The management team needs information to make broad-scope decisions. Hierarchical control is exercised by monitoring results and process indicators rather than by becoming involved in daily activities.

An equally robust lateral information system is also required. With such a system, people can work laterally with peers, and managers aren't necessary to mediate between teams.

PERFORMANCE INFORMATION

Performance information is particularly important.

Team members need real-time access to information about their team's performance on all dimensions. Sharing this information should not be seen as a manager's choice. Team members won't own team performance if they aren't expected to be aware of it.

The following performance information is especially important:

❑ The goals and priorities of the organization and its parts

❑ The plans for accomplishing the goals

❑ Ongoing feedback about results

This feedback links the teams to the bigger system that they're part of. It also provides a foundation for trade-offs and adjustments.

CUSTOMER INFORMATION

Sharing customer information has a particular importance:

❑ A key success factor for organizations is meeting customer requirements and providing services, products, and applications that are of value to the customer.

❑ The customer's viewpoint exists independent of the views of diverse organizational contributors.

A focus on customer concerns and preferences provides a common and neutral base of information that can help a team get beyond internal disagreements and concentrate on delivering value.

DRAFTING A NEW COMMUNICATION STRATEGY

PLANNING NEW INFORMATION ROUTES

New information routes have to be planned and formalized.

At the beginning, members of a team-based organization will not be in the habit of sharing all necessary information laterally. As the organization moves through a dynamic configuration of teams, the necessary information routes change.

The organization needs to identify these new communication routes and assign responsibilities:

❑ Team charters, described in detail in Module 8, should include communication responsibilities.

❑ Team plans should include approaches to fulfill communication responsibilities.

Teams can be held responsible for task-related communication with other work and support teams. They should also be formally responsible for reporting information to other teams such as improvement teams, the management team, and involvement teams—and for getting the information they themselves need from these teams. To meet these responsibilities, individuals in a team might be assigned as communication liaisons to other groups.

SUPPORTING INFORMATION AND COMMUNICATION NEEDS

The organization needs to support the information and communication needs of teams.

❑ **Information technology systems** should be designed to support new multidirectional communication links and information needs.

By systematizing the *sharing of information*, teams can make the most of their valuable face-to-face time—deliberating, solving problems, and making decisions.

Communication is everyone's responsibility

Management is responsible for the quality of the information systems in the organization and for making information widely available.

Everyone is responsible for sharing information and for being informed.

AVOIDING INFORMATION OVERLOAD

Information can be overwhelming. Electronic systems make it easy to copy everyone with everything.

The organization needs to develop strong guidelines to prevent people from being inundated with irrelevant information. For example:

❑ Make information accessible in such a way that people can quickly identify the information they need rather than sift through information they don't need.

❑ Tag information so people can quickly determine its relevance.

❑ Where possible, send information, not just data. Make data available as a backup.

People should talk as a group about the kind of information they need to share and the best way to share it to avoid overload.

ESTABLISHING COMMUNICATION NORMS

New behaviors are required to support the altered communication patterns in a team-based organization. Possible new norms are:

❑ Communication is open—information is broadly accessible rather than only on a "need-to-know" basis.

❑ Responsibility lies with individuals to make needed information available to others—*and* to monitor relevant information in the organization's communication system.

❑ Meetings are designed to collectively use information—whenever possible, information is shared in advance.

SOME SAMPLE INFORMATION ROUTES

The NPD process maps on page 2-6 show many of the communication links that need to be established for the sample organization. This example shows a few additional routes to illustrate some—though not all—of the additional communication needs in this new product development organization.

The first, necessitated by the establishment of a division-wide software-reuse team, is a means for the product design team to communicate its software designs to the reuse team. The reuse team can then create a software data base to share with product design teams in other NPD efforts. Other communication routes are necessary to develop IT systems that support the system needs of the NPD teams. A shared services team has also been created to support local IT system needs.

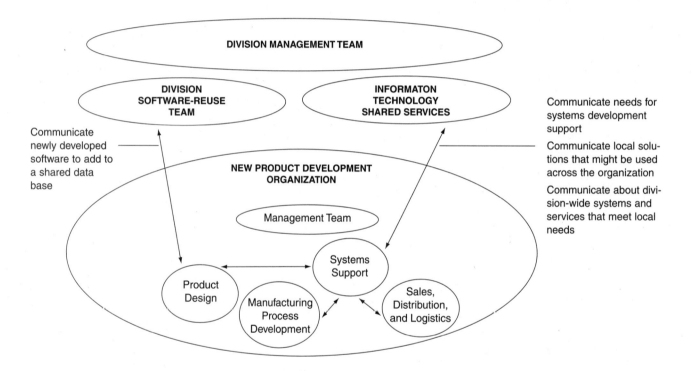

NPD INFORMATION APPROACHES

❑ Put the PERT chart, Cost Matrix, and other performance indicators on the system so team members can refer to it.

❑ Keep a running list of team issues and assignments so that people know whom to talk to as issues arise.

❑ Put all customer feedback on the local network for daily distribution and keep a running list of customer comments accessible to anyone on the team.

GENERAL COMMUNICATION NORMS

❑ It's the responsibility of all team members to efficiently make others aware of information that affects their work and is needed to be an informed team member.

❑ It's the responsibility of all team members to get the information they need to do their work and to be informed team members.

DRAFTING A NEW COMMUNICATION STRATEGY: WHAT TO DO

Sketch the organizational communication routes that need to be formalized and determine approaches that make them work. Then make your new communication norms explicit.

NEW COMMUNICATION ROUTES

NEW COMMUNICATION APPROACHES	NEW COMMUNICATION NORMS

WHAT'S NEXT

In this module, you've identified the nontraditional communication routes that need to be built into your team-based organization so people are well informed and can carry out their responsibilities and contribute to the organization as a whole.

You've also thought about systems that can be set up to assure that information sharing is built into the way you do business. You've identified the norms that should govern communication in your organization.

❑ You'll need to get input to these plans and help in executing them from your team members.

❑ You'll also need to model new communication norms and stress their importance.

Now you're ready to consider a process that's key to everyone's success: the way performance is managed in your team-based organization.

TO DO

MANAGING AND IMPROVING PERFORMANCE

ACTIVITY IN THIS MODULE

DESIGNING A
PERFORMANCE
MANAGEMENT SYSTEM

Performance management is a multifaceted activity in a team-based organization. It contributes most to performance if

❏ The performance requirements are defined for the business unit, its teams, and their members so that all share an understanding of how they fit in the bigger picture.

❏ Individuals, teams, and the organization are developed so that they are capable of performing as required.

❏ Performance is reviewed so that all know how they're doing and whether performance needs to be redefined or further development is necessary.

❏ Performance at all levels—individual, team, and business unit—is recognized and rewarded.

This module explains the full performance management cycle and its facets. Much of the discussion focuses on the performance management of teams and their members, but performance management has to occur at all levels of the organization.

THE PERFORMANCE MANAGEMENT CYCLE

Managing performance is an ongoing cycle that shapes the work done in the organization. Performance management happens through

- ❑ Formal processes such as goal setting and performance appraisal

- ❑ Informal processes as teams go about doing their work in a systematic manner

Formal practices may occur in yearly or quarterly cycles or according to natural performance periods such as product development cycles and milestones. Informal practices are ongoing.

LEVELS OF PERFORMANCE MANAGEMENT

In a team-based organization, all phases of the performance management cycle need to be carried out for all the performing entities:

- ❑ The business unit as a whole

- ❑ The teams that compose it

- ❑ The individuals who make up the teams

Through the performance management processes, performance at all these levels of the organizational system is aligned and improved.

Performance management at the team level and business-unit level shapes the delivery of products and services, providing goals, feedback, incentives, and capability improvement.

Team-level performance management practices are particularly important for effective team performance.

Individual-level performance management is best conducted within the context of team and organizational goals.

```
                 Planning and Goal-
                   Setting Systems

                       Defining

  Reward                                    Development and
  Systems    Rewarding  Performance  Developing   Allocation Systems

                      Reviewing

                 Appraisal and
                 Review Systems
```

Performance management is a cycle of definition and development, reviews, and rewards

IT'S EVERYONE'S RESPONSIBILITY

In the traditional organization, performance management and performance improvement are the responsibility of the management hierarchy. In the team-based organization, these functions occur laterally as well.

Self-management occurs when members of performing units—business units and teams—assume responsibility for managing and improving their own performance as units. Hierarchy doesn't completely disappear, though:

❑ The team's performance management is carried out in the context of the business unit's direction and performance needs.

❑ Individual performance management is carried out in the context of the team's mission and performance requirements.

The management team orchestrates overall performance management, using the direction-setting processes in Module 4 as an important part of defining performance requirements. In addition, the management team needs to ensure that processes for multilevel goal setting, reviews, rewards, and development are in place—and that they are contributing to the kinds of performance required for business success.

TEAMS HAVE MULTIPLE STAKEHOLDERS

A performance management plan needs to take into account multiple viewpoints, including those of:

❑ Co-workers

❑ Other teams and units that are interdependent

❑ Customers

❑ The business, as represented by higher-level management teams

Each of these stakeholders has its own expectations of the team's performance. When the performance management process includes input from all of these perspectives, everyone in the organization grapples with all the dimensions of performance.

To achieve ownership at all levels, performance management practices have to be highly participative.

DEFINING PERFORMANCE

DELINEATING THE WORK

The defining processes in performance management shape the work to be done. They include:

- ❑ Mission and roles
- ❑ Goals and objectives
- ❑ Identification of stakeholder needs
- ❑ Deliverables, milestones, and tasks to be accomplished
- ❑ Metrics
- ❑ Planning
- ❑ Identification of resources needed

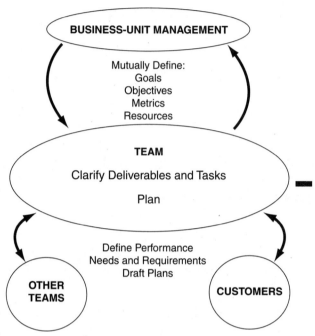

Processes that define team performance requirements are carried out by the team in interaction with its management, its customers, and other teams...

Definition is the foundation for all performance management

A clear definition of performance requirements establishes common understanding.

This definition has the greatest impact on actual performance.

The effectiveness of other aspects—reviews, development, and rewards—depends on having the definition in place.

...and provide a context for defining individual performance requirements.

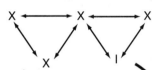

TEAM

Participates in Defining
Goals, Objectives, Metrics

Assesses Resource Availability

Plans Application of Resources to Tasks

MEMBERS

X ←→ X ←→ X
X   I

Mutually Define Each Member's
Role and Contribution

MEMBER I

Combines Roles and
Expected Contributions
to Team or Teams into
Overall Definition of
Own Performance

GOALS AND PLANS ARE LIVING DOCUMENTS

Goals and plans have to be tracked and revised as needed.

In the traditional organization, managers track them and make changes in individual assignments accordingly.

In a team-based organization, work is done laterally, and team members have to be aware of where they are with respect to goals and plans. They have to watch for changing conditions that require alterations in the goals and plans of the team and its members.

EXAMPLE:
AN APPROACH TO DEFINING PERFORMANCE

The direction-setting process discussed in Module 4 is a major component of defining performance. An important addition to direction setting is the determination of capability needs and plans for development. In this example, the organization has created a performance management involvement team (PMIT) to oversee many of the processes.

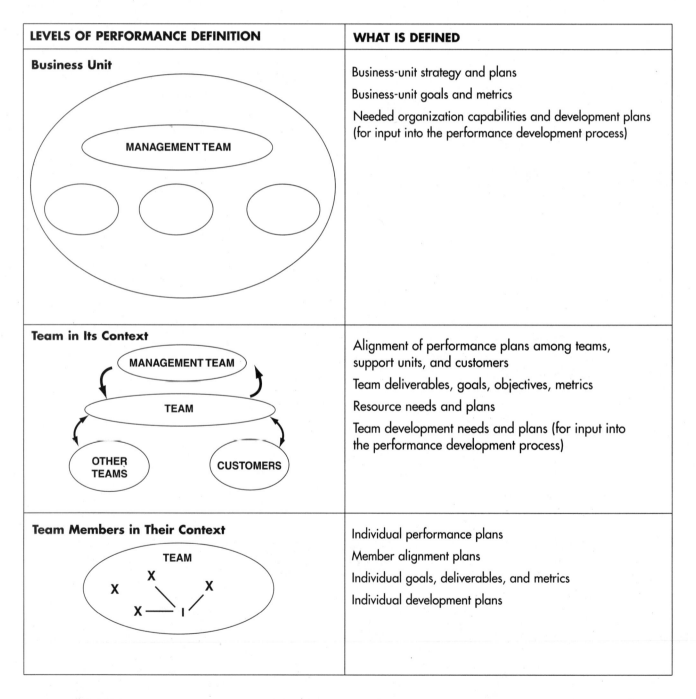

LEVELS OF PERFORMANCE DEFINITION	WHAT IS DEFINED
Business Unit MANAGEMENT TEAM	Business-unit strategy and plans Business-unit goals and metrics Needed organization capabilities and development plans (for input into the performance development process)
Team in Its Context MANAGEMENT TEAM TEAM OTHER TEAMS CUSTOMERS	Alignment of performance plans among teams, support units, and customers Team deliverables, goals, objectives, metrics Resource needs and plans Team development needs and plans (for input into the performance development process)
Team Members in Their Context TEAM X X X X X I	Individual performance plans Member alignment plans Individual goals, deliverables, and metrics Individual development plans

WHO PARTICIPATES	HOW DEFINING IS DONE
The PMIT has responsibility for managing the process, although the management team and other teams remain the main actors and decision makers. The management team makes substantive determinations. Teams provide input.	Consensually, starting with input from teams and support units and with the strategy and plans of the larger organization (see Module 4 example) Yearly determination of goals and plans, including development plans, quarterly updates Quarterly updates

Team
PMIT facilitates the process as requested.
 	
Other participants include:
  Work teams
  Customers
  Integration teams
  Management team
	Yearly iterative process within each team in interaction with other interdependent units and the management team
	
	Dialogues among teams and customers
	
	Contracting processes
	
	Reviewed as needed

Team members	Team meetings Discussions with key co-workers and customers Yearly, but reviewed as needed

REVIEWING PERFORMANCE

EVALUATING REQUIREMENTS

Performance reviews determine whether performance is delivering value and meeting the requirements of the situation. Reviews include:

❑ Feedback from stakeholders

❑ Assessment of performance against targets

❑ Determination of ways to improve performance

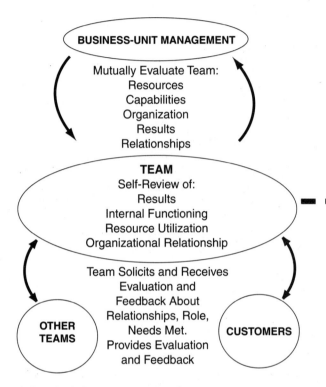

Each level of the organization has its own responsibilities for team review

> ### Team review is essential
>
> Regular review of team performance is particularly key. It focuses attention on how well a team is doing at carrying out a whole piece of the work that delivers value to customers. It makes members aware that they must focus on more than their own individual performance.
>
> Review does not, in and of itself, lead to better performance. Further performance definition and development of new approaches and capabilities do that.

PUTTING REVIEWS TO WORK

Performance reviews feed into all aspects of performance management. They:

❑ Serve as the basis for revising and updating work definitions

❑ Trigger the identification of problem areas that need attention and opportunities for development and improvement

❑ Provide a foundation for performance-based recognition and reward

Individuals participate in reviews of the team, their peers, and their own work

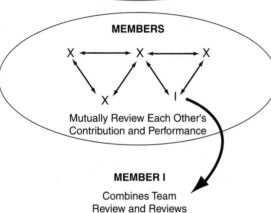

TEAM

Compiles Reviews from Managers, Customers, Other Teams

Reviews Members as Part of Its Self-Review

Shares Reviews

MEMBERS

Mutually Review Each Other's Contribution and Performance

MEMBER I

Combines Team Review and Reviews from Other Teams into Overall Performance Review

EXAMPLE:
AN APPROACH TO PERFORMANCE REVIEW

LEVELS OF PERFORMANCE REVIEW	WHAT IS REVIEWED
Business Unit (diagram: large ellipse containing MANAGEMENT TEAM ellipse above three smaller ellipses)	Assessment of business performance—financial, market, productivity, industry, for example—vis-à-vis goals, metrics, and mission Identification of organization functioning, improvement needs, and development efforts Customer satisfaction
Team in Its Context (diagram: MANAGEMENT TEAM at top, TEAM in middle, OTHER TEAMS and CUSTOMERS at bottom, connected by arrows)	Assessment of team/unit performance in terms of metrics, goals, targets, customer satisfaction, and costs Identification of improvement needs for team Assessment of linkages among team and units Identification of requirements for improving team and interteam linkages (input into the development process)
Team Members in Their Context (diagram: ellipse labeled TEAM containing X marks connected to an "I")	Assessment and feedback of individual contributions Identification of individual development needs and plans

WHO PARTICIPATES	HOW THE REVIEW IS DONE
PMIT initiates the review, gathers information, and oversees the process. Management team does substantive reviewing. Teams give input.	*Monthly:* Performance data are compiled. Management team interprets the data. Management team shares status with all members. *Quarterly:* Input is collected from team, interteam, and customer assessments.
Teams review themselves and give input to reviews of other teams and support units. PMIT oversees the process. Management team reviews teams. Customers give input.	*Quarterly:* Management team oversees team and interteam review processes. Management team formally reviews the team process, results, and plans. Team surveys other work teams, support units, and integration teams. Team surveys customers (assessment aimed at team, not individuals). *Monthly:* Members review performance data. Members discuss and plan performance-improvement strategies. *Yearly:* Review feeds into performance bonus decision.
Team reviews Team members give self-reviews and input to reviews of others. Other key contacts give assessment input.	*Quarterly:* Co-workers assess performance using adapted version of corporate performance-appraisal form. *Yearly:* Individuals receive a formal review—a compendium of assessments from co-workers and others who were key contacts. Team reviews and recommends development plans. Team may recommend individual bonuses.

REWARDING PERFORMANCE

LINKING REWARDS TO THE PERFORMANCE MANAGEMENT CYCLE

Reward systems direct activity by sending strong messages about what is valued in the organization.

If people believe they will receive rewards for performing in certain well-defined ways, they will endeavor to do so. Performance-based rewards complement the defining and reviewing processes of performance management. The impact of rewards on performance is strongest if:

❑ The organization spends time defining what performance is needed and its organizational priorities

❑ The organization spends time reviewing how it is doing and making plans to enhance performance

In the absence of clear definition and processes for ongoing feedback and improvement, rewards lose much of their motivational impact.

REWARDING AT ALL LEVELS

Rewards focus effort. At each level in the organization, rewards focus effort differently:

❑ Rewards based on team performance or on contributions to the team focus effort on the product or service that the team delivers.

❑ Rewards based on business-unit performance focus effort on interactions across the organization that are required for systemwide performance.

❑ Rewards based on individual contribution allow people to feel valued. Individual rewards can detract from team performance if they pit team members against each other or if they are perceived as unfair—or if they reward activities that deflect attention from the team's goals.

Performance and compensation

Linking compensation to performance creates a direct stake in performance. Performance-based compensation is particularly motivating if people feel they have control over the variables leading to performance.

BUILDING RECOGNITION
AND SPECIAL REWARDS

Motivating environments have lots of routes to positive personal outcomes.

In a traditional organization, hierarchical promotions are the main mechanism for acknowledging contributions. In a flat organization, there are fewer opportunities for such promotions. So it's particularly important for team-based organizations to create many ways to acknowledge the contribution of teams and of people within them.

Formal recognition programs should include giving team members the power to recognize and award each other, other teams, and individuals outside the team who have contributed to performance.

In addition to formal recognition programs, day-to-day informal behavior is also critical. Managers need to model the behavior of acknowledging and expressing appreciation for good performance and hard work. But this behavior also needs to become commonplace throughout the organization.

Equity in a team-based system

At first, people who are accustomed to individual rewards in the traditional organization may not feel equitably treated if their rewards are based on team and organizational performance.

Equity will increase as people:

❑ Operate and are truly treated as members of interdependent teams

❑ Understand the reward system

❑ Get involved in group efforts to improve performance

❑ Participate in all phases of performance management

EXAMPLE:
AN APPROACH TO REWARDING PERFORMANCE

In this example, rewards are determined based on performance as measured during reviews. Rewards are distributed based on the performance of the business and the team and on the contribution of the individual.

LEVELS OF REWARDED PERFORMANCE	REWARDS FOR BUSINESS-UNIT PERFORMANCE
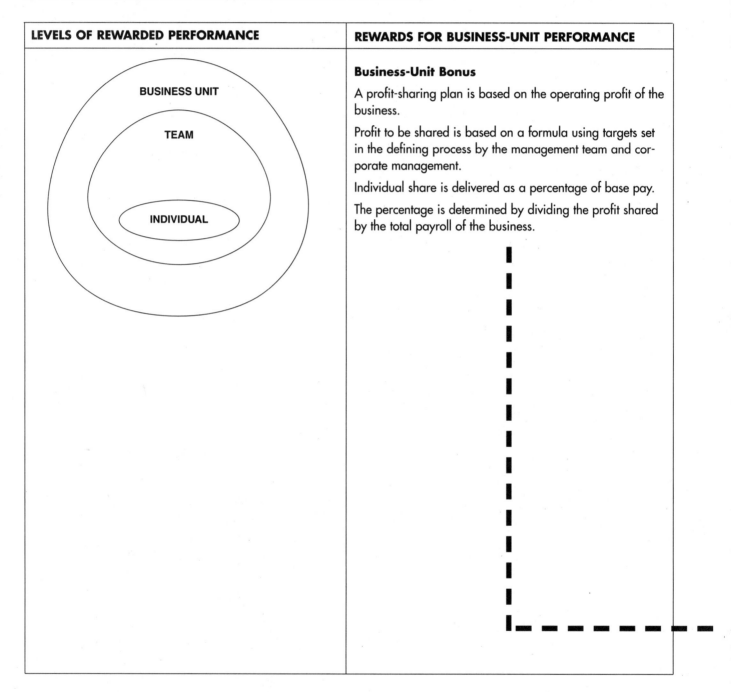	**Business-Unit Bonus** A profit-sharing plan is based on the operating profit of the business. Profit to be shared is based on a formula using targets set in the defining process by the management team and corporate management. Individual share is delivered as a percentage of base pay. The percentage is determined by dividing the profit shared by the total payroll of the business.

REWARDS FOR TEAM PERFORMANCE	REWARDS FOR INDIVIDUAL CONTRIBUTIONS

Team Bonus

A quality-productivity bonus plan is based on an established formula for team performance that includes customer ratings, ratings by the management team, ratings by other teams with which the team must work, and especially targets and metrics set during the defining process.

Ratings are never determined by ranking teams against one another; they are based on predetermined dimensions of performance.

All members of a team receive an equal team portion of the team bonus.

Performance Bonus

Bonuses based on individual performance are given only to those who are consensually rated by their peers as especially deserving, given their performance. This will be rare, and it is expected that often no one will be given an individual performance bonus.

Teams apply for member bonuses from a business-unit pool.

Competency-Based Pay

Base pay of individuals is based on the market worth of the person's skills as well as the worth to the business of certain business-specific skills.

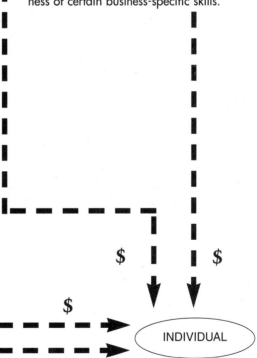

DEVELOPING AND IMPROVING

DEVELOPING THE ABILITY TO WORK LATERALLY

In the traditional organization, the development portion of performance management focuses largely on individual competencies.

Development in a team-based organization also focuses on team and organizational capabilities. It includes developing organizational arrangements and practices:

❑ Acquiring and allocating the resources necessary for performance

❑ Developing team processes, work arrangements, and roles for effective performance

❑ Establishing effective relationships with customers, suppliers, and other teams

❑ Improving work methods, tools, systems, and processes

❑ Ensuring the development of competencies in the short and long term

INTRODUCING SYSTEMWIDE IMPROVEMENTS

Improvement teams often introduce improvements that contribute to systemwide performance. For example, they might introduce

❑ New computer systems for tracking projects

❑ New approaches to competency development that move people through a succession of assignments that cut across teams

❑ New systems and processes for software reuse across the organization

Systemwide performance improvement depends on the adoption of these approaches across the organization. Therefore, team responsibility for using new approaches needs to be clarified in the team charter and goals.

IMPROVING TEAMS FROM WITHIN

Teams need to continually improve and change the way they do work in order to accomplish their objectives through time. Team self-improvement occurs when team members are involved in

❑ Reviewing the performance of the team

❑ Discussing ways to perform more effectively

Sharing performance information helps the team know where it needs to put its effort. Performance capabilities improve when the team takes the time to actively review performance information and formulate plans to change how it operates in order to get back on track or to be able to meet increasingly difficult goals.

The leadership role

Two benefits of a team-based organization are

❑ The local generation of new ways of organizing and interacting

❑ New approaches to using team resources

A key leadership task in a team-based organization is to lead the process by which team members systematically look at better ways to do their work.

EXAMPLE:
AN APPROACH TO DEVELOPMENT AND IMPROVEMENT

LEVELS OF DEVELOPMENT AND IMPROVEMENT	WHAT IS DEVELOPED AND IMPROVED
Business Unit MANAGEMENT TEAM	Design of the organization Technology infrastructure Training and development systems to develop needed competencies Other organizational systems Resource allocation Measurement systems and metrics
Team in Its Context MANAGEMENT TEAM TEAM OTHER TEAMS CUSTOMERS	Team structure and design Acquisition of needed tools and equipment Acquisition of needed skills Team procedures and infrastructure Resource allocation and assignment Interteam linkages and infrastructures Development of relationships and interfaces among teams and customers
Team Members in Their Context TEAM X X X X — I	Member skills and knowledge

WHO PARTICIPATES	HOW DEVELOPMENT IS DONE
PMIT may initiate. Management team oversees development of the organization. Various improvement/design teams get involved in particular development efforts.	Organization-wide development and improvement processes as necessary—based on results of defining and reviewing processes System design and implementation Organization-wide training Organization redesign activities
Work teams Customers Improvement teams Management team	Yearly planning session to apply results of review and to determine new team processes and roles One team meeting per month dedicated to improvement of team practices Relationship building with other teams and customers—based on results of team review process and meetings with interdependent groups to develop new linking mechanisms and operating practices Equipment purchases Self-design process for teams at transition points
Team members Team as a whole	On-the-job training and cross-training Formal training

DESIGNING A PERFORMANCE MANAGEMENT SYSTEM: WHAT TO DO

Use the information and examples in this module to sketch the outlines of a performance management approach that makes sense given the design choices you've already made.

DEFINING	DEVELOPING AND IMPROVING
Business unit **Who:** **What:** **How:**	*Business unit* **Who:** **What:** **How:**
Team in its context **Who:** **What:** **How:**	*Team in its context* **Who:** **What:** **How:**
Team members in their context **Who:** **What:** **How:**	*Team members in their context* **Who:** **What:** **How:**

© Jossey-Bass, Inc.

REVIEWING	REWARDING
Business unit	*Business-unit rewards*
Who:	
What:	
How:	
Team in its context	*Team-level rewards*
Who:	
What:	
How:	
Team members in their context	*Individual-level rewards*
Who:	
What:	
How:	

WHAT'S NEXT

In this module, you've sketched the outlines of a performance management approach.

Many details still need to be worked out—not the least of which is how this approach can be made to work within the larger corporation.

Many of your new practices may be incompatible with existing practices and philosophy. Your performance improvement efforts may need to begin by addressing these incompatibilities.

Or you may be able to modify organizational approaches by

❑ Adding peer input to individual performance management systems

❑ Conducting formal team performance management practices

❑ Stressing the alignment of individual team and business-unit performance management

Now you're ready to look at the issues of authority and responsibility in the team-based organization—the process of chartering teams. Module 8 guides you through this process.

TO DO

ESTABLISHING THE TEAM CHARTER

ACTIVITIES IN THIS MODULE

DEFINING BUSINESS-UNIT CHARTERS

DEFINING TEAM CHARTERS

Team-based organizations place responsibility and authority in a variety of performing units, often with unique configurations. To clearly define these configurations, the organization needs a charter for itself and for each of its teams.

The chartering process creates a shared set of expectations for how the organization will operate:

❑ It begins the alignment process.

❑ It determines the domain of each team.

❑ It creates an explicit understanding of authority and responsibility.

This module guides you through the process of creating charters for different kinds of teams.

CHARTERING TEAMS

CREATING SHARED UNDERSTANDING

In team-based organizations, responsibility and authority aren't built into a well-defined hierarchy and departmental system. They're embodied in a unique configuration of performing units, designed specifically to fit the work of the organization.

A chartering process creates shared understanding:

❑ It creates common expectations about domains. Without charters, things fall between the cracks, and there is redundancy.

❑ It minimizes confusion and ambiguity about boundaries and authority. Without clear charters, such ambiguity can impede the integrated functioning of the organization.

❑ It supports lateral processes and empowerment. Without charters, managers often end up adjudicating between teams.

A complete charter specifies outcome and process requirements, resources available to the team, authority, constraints, and linking mechanisms.

CHARTERING AT ALL LEVELS

Chartering should occur at various levels. Business units should be chartered, and each team and unit within them should be chartered.

Chartering defines the relationships among performing units:

❑ It lays out domains of responsibility clearly.

❑ It begins the process of alignment by specifying a team's mission and goals in the context of the organization's mission and goals.

❑ It creates an explicit description of authority, responsibility, and accountability.

Even the management team needs a charter to clarify its role within the business unit. The role of managers is often ambiguous in a new team-based organization. Teams expect more autonomy than is possible given the integrated nature of the organization. Managers may be uncertain about when and how to influence teams. A charter for the management team helps clarify—for everyone—the role that management can be expected to play.

SHARING CHARTERS

Charters and changes to charters should be broadly shared.

Members of the organization have to develop a shared understanding of the organization and how it's intended to operate. Sharing team charters

❑ Gives people a picture of the organizational system that helps them to operate effectively within it

❑ Ensures that people within each team and across teams have the same understanding of who's doing what

GETTING INPUT IN THE CHARTERING PROCESS

The management team has the primary responsibility for the chartering process. The charter is the management team's tool for

❑ Describing how the organization will operate as a system

❑ Making sure that the resources of the organization are being applied effectively to carry out the organization's mission.

However, teams are more likely to accept their charters if they have influence in creating them. Teams also need to be able to initiate clarification of charters with other teams. Input and negotiation are desirable and necessary in the chartering process.

Chartering should be a two-way process

Managers specify the mission of the team, its resources, and how it relates to broader organizational strategy and goals.

The team itself can think through and create a draft charter, including team goals, stakeholder expectations, integration requirements, and appropriate escalation paths.

Together, they can review and finalize the charter, adding the processes that will be used to review the team regularly.

EXAMPLE:
CHARTER FOR A SOFTWARE INTEGRATING TEAM

1 BROAD ORGANIZATIONAL GOALS

Division goals
- Return profit after investment of 7% of sales.
- Achieve 95% on-time delivery and attainment of milestones, 87% superior rating from customers, 97% quality index, 25% software reusability index.
- Implement an electronic lessons-learned file.
- Implement groupware for program management and coordination.

Program goals
- Return profit of 9% of revenue.
- Achieve 100% on-time delivery and attainment of milestones, superior ratings at five milestone points, 99% quality index, 30% software reuse.
- Achieve follow-on enhancement program funding (goal shared with proposal team). Implement and use groupware for program management.
- Achieve full concurrency of development of three components.
- Strive for rapid iteration and minimal rework.

2 MISSION OF TEAM

Products and services, including support to other teams and units
To assure that the software in the program works as a high-quality integrated system and is developed efficiently within budget and quality specs. Specifically:
- Make final decisions regarding overall software architecture
- Make trade-offs that involve software being developed in each of the three teams: Component I, Component II, and Subcontracted Software Development
- Assure documentation of all changes and immediate communication (by groupware) of all changes
- Manage relationship with external contractor

3 TEAM GOALS

- Achieve six major program milestones on schedule and within budget (joint goals with the three contributing work teams).
- Always convene—electronically if necessary—to resolve cross-team architecture decisions within 24 hours of request.
- Use 30% of software from previous program (joint with work teams).
- Make documentation at each milestone available to other programs.

4 STAKEHOLDERS AND THEIR KEY EXPECTATIONS

Customers
Timely milestone documentation and timely notification and involvement in changes to specifications for prime contractor

The business (management)
- Up-to-date project performance data
- Timely notification of problems, overruns
- Contribution to lessons-learned system
- Implementation of groupware and contribution to divisional learning

Other teams and units
Components I and II and External Contractor:
- Resolution of key trade-offs after receiving high-level plans
- Timely resolution of ongoing integration decisions; monitoring and detecting integration problems and convening of parties involved for resolution
- Scanning output from other programs to find reusable code
- Timely information

Suppliers (including support services)
Groupware implementation team: timely adherence to implementation and training schedule and feedback about bugs and learnings

External contractor: See "Other teams and units"

5 RESOURCES

People
- 15% of time of six software engineers and two systems engineers
- 10% of quality engineer, with services to be provided in preparation for each milestone

Budget
- People as targeted
- Travel — six trips per month to and from contractor site
- Work stations and software

6 ESCALATION PATH

- Unresolved issues are escalated to the program management team.
- Example of such an issue: hardware/software trade-offs and reuse decisions that have negative implications for schedule and cost targets.

7 REQUIREMENTS FOR INTEGRATION WITH OTHER GROUPS

- Members coordinate with the work team that they represent on the software integrating team.
- One member is assigned to link to six other programs with related software content.
- One member serves on the "lessons-learned" improvement team and another on the performance management involvement team.

8 REVIEW PROCESSES

- Software subsystem activity reviewed at each milestone by the program management team.
- Integrating team self-reviews monthly with quarterly input from each of the three teams being integrated.
- Quarterly review of integrating team by program management team to make sure it is meeting program needs.

DEFINING BUSINESS-UNIT CHARTERS:
WHAT TO DO

First, identify the key aspects of a charter for your business unit. This charter creates the context for chartering each team within it.

1 BROAD ORGANIZATIONAL GOALS	2 MISSION OF BUSINESS UNIT
The larger organization	Products and services, including support to other teams and units:

3 BUSINESS-UNIT GOALS	4 STAKEHOLDERS AND THEIR KEY EXPECTATIONS
	Customers
	The larger organization (management)
	Other teams and business units
	Suppliers (including support services)

5 RESOURCES	6 ESCALATION PATH
People	
Budget	

7 REQUIREMENTS FOR INTEGRATION WITH OTHER GROUPS	8 REVIEW PROCESSES

DEFINING TEAM CHARTERS:
WHAT TO DO

Now identify the key elements of the charter for at least one team within the business unit.

Don't choose the management team for this exercise. You'll develop its charter in Module 9.

You will eventually need a charter for every team in your business unit.

1 BROAD ORGANIZATIONAL GOALS	2 MISSION OF TEAM
	Products and services, including support to other teams and units:

3 TEAM GOALS	4 STAKEHOLDERS AND THEIR KEY EXPECTATIONS
	Customers
	The larger organization (management)
	Other teams and business units
	Suppliers (including support services)

5 RESOURCES	6 ESCALATION PATH
People	
Budget	

7 REQUIREMENTS FOR INTEGRATION WITH OTHER GROUPS	8 REVIEW PROCESSES

WHAT'S NEXT

With this module, you've begun the process of chartering your team-based organization. This process is not complete until all teams have been chartered.

You'll want to get team involvement in the chartering process. However, the key parameters of team charters—mission and resources—have to be specified by the management team that is responsible for

❏ Setting direction

❏ Allocating resources

❏ Designing a configuration of units that can carry out the mission of the business unit

❏ Aligning these units

You'll need to develop a way to share all charters so people have a common understanding of how the organization is intended to operate.

The next module provides a summary framework for understanding the responsibility of management in a team-based organization. You'll charter the management team in that module.

TO DO

_____
_____
_____
_____
_____
_____
_____
_____
_____
_____
_____
_____
_____
_____
_____
_____
_____
_____
_____
_____
_____
_____
_____

LEADING A TEAM-BASED ORGANIZATION

ACTIVITIES IN THIS MODULE

CHARTERING THE
MANAGEMENT TEAM

SUMMARIZING AND
SYNTHESIZING

This module provides a framework for thinking about the ongoing responsibilities of the management team in a team-based organization. In many companies, this team is called the leadership team.

The management team, whether composed of hierarchical managers or representatives, needs to have a clear image of its role in the organization. In this module, you'll charter the management team.

You'll also review the work you've done in designing your team-based organization and work through a checklist for

❑ Structures and processes

❑ Team functions

❑ Ownership and accountability

❑ Norms

❑ Opportunities for growth and development

CHARTERING THE MANAGEMENT TEAM

ENABLING A LATERAL ORGANIZATION TO FUNCTION

The management team creates the context in which teams and other forms of lateral integration can operate effectively. Its role is to

❑ Provide overall strategic direction and align the organization

❑ Ensure that teams and units are configured to efficiently and effectively perform the work of the organization

❑ Monitor the team configuration and make changes through time as the mix of work changes

❑ Make sure the organization has the systems necessary to support the team-based processes

❑ Orchestrate a performance management process that keeps all performing units aligned and focused on the performance needs of the organization—and on improving performance capabilities

❑ Model team behavior and the norms that are important in a team organization

❑ Remove barriers and break logjams to enable teams to function effectively

In short, the management team provides direction and builds organizational capability. It spends more time leading and developing the organization and less time overseeing work than in the traditional hierarchical organization.

DEVELOPING THE TEAM-BASED ORGANIZATION

In organizations that are in transition to a lateral, team-oriented mode of operating, the management team leads the learning process and helps the organization gradually develop the capabilities for lateral functioning. It does so by:

❑ Engaging in learning processes to become a more effective leadership team

❑ Planning and leading a gradual transfer of management tasks as teams develop the capability for self-management

❑ Coaching leaders and teams as they learn a new way of operating

❑ Regularly assessing the capabilities of the organization—and intervening to develop the organization

❑ Encouraging teams to review their own capabilities and engage in learning-oriented activities

❑ Establishing and formalizing team-based practices and systems so that they are not dependent on the discretion of individual managers

LEADING THE LEARNING PROCESS

A learning organization is one that gets better at operating in the new way over time. It's an organization where continuous performance improvement is the norm.

To develop a learning organization, the management team can lead the way by actively promoting

❏ Dialogue and reflection to develop a shared understanding of how the team-based organization works

❏ Team-building activities designed to help teams determine how they will operate

❏ Team self-reviews of performance and planning for improvement

❏ Exchange of learnings across teams and across organizations

❏ Skill building

REVIEWING RESULTS AND PROCESSES

The management team models a focus on results and on organizational and team processes.

❏ Regular review of team and organizational processes is key to the development of increased performance capabilities.

Continuous improvement depends on increasing lateral competencies and using the new organization to perform better.

What remains to be done

You have one final design task—to charter the management team.

In addition, you need to review the entire design—using a list to check your work.

You'll do these two tasks on the next four pages.

CHARTERING THE MANAGEMENT TEAM:
WHAT TO DO

The management team has a special set of responsibilities to help the business unit accomplish its business objectives. Create a charter for carrying out these responsibilities.

1 BROAD ORGANIZATIONAL GOALS	2 MISSION OF TEAM
The larger organization	*For example:*
	To establish direction and develop the
	capability of the business unit
The business unit	

3 GOALS	4 STAKEHOLDERS AND THEIR KEY EXPECTATIONS
	Customers
	The larger organization (management)
	Other teams and business units
	Suppliers (including support services)
	Employees

5 RESOURCES	6 ESCALATION PATH
People	
Budget	

7 REQUIREMENTS FOR INTEGRATION WITH OTHER GROUPS	8 REVIEW PROCESSES

SUMMARIZING AND SYNTHESIZING:
WHAT TO DO

In this book, you've created the plans for an effective team-based organization.

Use this checklist to review and discuss what you've done—and to make sure your plans meet the requirements of an effective team-based organization.

DOES YOUR DESIGN ...	IF NOT, HOW CAN YOU IMPROVE IT?
HAVE STRUCTURES THAT FIT THE WORK?	
Work teams	
Integrating teams	
Improvement and involvement teams	
A process for reviewing structures as the work mix,	
goals, and strategies change	
CREATE CONDITIONS FOR TEAM OWNERSHIP AND	
ACCOUNTABILITY?	
Clear direction	
Clear charters	
Team management of and accountability for	
all aspects of performance	
Capability development	
Common fate and outcomes	
DEFINE EFFECTIVE PROCESSES?	
For working cross-functionally	
For aligning goals	
For communicating	
For lateral decision making	
For learning	
For systematic work	

DOES YOUR DESIGN ...	IF NOT, HOW CAN YOU IMPROVE IT?
VEST APPROPRIATE FUNCTIONS IN TEAMS?	
Planning	
Coordination and integration of work	
Self management of performance	
Improvement	
Managing boundaries	
Effective utilization of resources	
FOSTER APPROPRIATE NORMS?	
Sharing information openly	
Valuing diverse perspectives	
Learning and improving	
Focusing on optimizing the whole system	
PROVIDE OPPORTUNITIES FOR GROWTH AND	
DEVELOPMENT OF MEMBERS?	
Broaden knowledge and skills	
Deepen knowledge and skills (where appropriate)	
Perform leadership functions	
Assume new roles	
WHAT ELSE?	
For example: Conflict resolution	
Integration of new team members	

WHAT'S NEXT

In this book, you've worked through a set of activities that helped you plan a foundation for your team-based organization.

You now need to get the input of others in the organization and develop a shared understanding of how the organization is going to operate:

- ❑ Talk about the framework you've developed.
- ❑ Regularly remind the organization of your expectations.
- ❑ Help the organization make it a reality.

Gradually, people will learn new ways of thinking and acting, and the new logic will guide the organization's work.

The team-based organization is not static. Over time, your team-based organization will continue to develop its capabilities and learn to become more effective. This learning won't happen automatically, though. To make it happen, you need to

- ❑ Establish the practice of regularly assessing how things are going
- ❑ Continue to make alterations and enhancements

Time spent building the capabilities of the team-based organization is time spent increasing performance.

NEXT STEPS

_____
_____
_____
_____
_____
_____

YET TO DO

_____
_____
_____
_____
_____
_____
_____
_____
_____
_____
_____
_____
_____